D0455158

PLATFORM

CYNTHIA JOHNSON

THE ART AND SCIENCE
OF PERSONAL BRANDING

LORENA JONES BOOKS
An imprint of **TEN SPEED PRESS**
California | New York

CONTENTS

TRUTH BE TOLD

When we begin to build a platform, we have a focus. Just as you need to lay the foundation before you can add the floor of a house, you need to lay the foundation of who you are before you can layer on top of it. We start out knowing exactly what we know and what we are okay with saying and to whom. As the platform grows and the audience expands, and as we become more comfortable in our position, we can then add to the house.

Once we have built our platform and people start to notice, we are given many new types of opportunities that can cloud our direction. Many people will ask us to tweet messages that don't fit who we are, to be interviewed on topics that we may or may not understand, and to be an influence on or the face of matters we aren't interested in. This is what causes platform fatigue. When we build a brand and stray from the message without a plan or purpose, we fatigue our audiences and ourselves.

As I started building my following and my influence online, I discovered that I could get into many meeting rooms, in front of many audiences, and be invited to speak on a range of topics— not because I was uniquely qualified in every subject but because I could deliver the message from a unique perspective. I was being used as a tool to spread messages. The most frustrating part was that it didn't matter what I said. Oftentimes, the interest wasn't due to my message or focus, but rather, to my audience and its reach. I found myself speaking in live televised interviews on major networks in five countries, on topics such as artificial intelligence, government regulation, international affairs, women's rights, and, of course, the 2016 United States elections.

At first it was interesting. I have experience in areas that allow me to have a perspective. However, it became concerning when I started to realize that other people were following along. Many people were hanging on my every word, which made me feel disingenuous. My opinion on government regulations in advanced technology was just that—my opinion—and I knew it shouldn't be taken as truth.

As I watched the 2016 US presidential election and the responses afterward, I saw that people were looking to validate their opinions when they should have been confirming their facts instead. This realization led me to ask, Who *are* the experts? And *where* are they?

My goal in writing this book is to encourage the real experts, the careerists, to start laying the foundation for their platforms, if not for themselves, then for the world. There is so much noise coming from so many people and places that we are exhausting the public attention span for experts and important causes. We need to hear from the people who understand topics completely and thoroughly. *Platform* is about you and your expertise, your reputation, and your influence. You can change the world with your voice if you have a platform to stand on and people who will listen.

So why am *I* the expert to write this book? Let me introduce myself: I am Cynthia Johnson, or as you may know me, @CynthiaLIVE. I have 1.7 million followers on Twitter. (I even have the blue check mark on Twitter and Instagram.) Mashable says I am the third-most important marketer to follow on Snapchat (@CyninLA); *Entrepreneur* magazine says I am one of the top five personal branding experts, and *Inc.* confirms that I am the twelfth-most-influential person when it comes to shifting marketing budgets and keeping chief information officers informed. *Adweek* thinks that I am one of the top marketers whom venture capitalists should be following. Basically, I am awesome and an expert at everything (insert some kind of hashtag here). I am kidding, of course. I am not an expert at everything, nor am I even a fan of the word *expert*, but I am a recognized digital marketing and personal branding professional.

As you read how I accomplished it all, you'll start to understand why the way I got here—and the mind-set required—matters. I worked hard, earned my reputation along the way, and took huge risks to get where I am, but many people have done the same without ever gaining substantial recognition or realizing new opportunities. My career was born out of a combination of being in the right place at the right time, having strong mentors, and necessity. The truth is, no matter how you look at it, all roads point to one main decision that launched my career and set me up for success: I created a personal brand.

Establishing a personal brand has enabled me to become a writer for major publications and to speak at various events and conferences, such as the Global Ventures Summit, Alibaba's Golden Bull Awards, the PR News conference, and the GetGlobal conference, to name a few. I am on the executive advisory board as well as a coach for Fortune 1000 executives (there are only twenty of us, and some are C-suite executives at companies such as Aetna). On occasion, I have the opportunity to travel around the world to work as an advisor. Have you ever heard of the World Marketing Congress or the World Government Summit? I had not heard of them either—until I was invited and flown to Dubai, China, Portugal, Bali, India, Turkey, and Israel to meet with government leaders, local experts, and philanthropists.

I have grown my following to nearly three million people across all social channels. I have spoken at nearly seventy-five events for different industries on various topics, in twenty-five states and seventeen countries—all in less than three years. I have been mentioned and featured in several major publications and blogs. I have become a go-to marketing and branding expert for some of the largest start-ups and venture capitalists in Silicon Valley and Los Angeles and have been able to monetize my brand without losing my authenticity. I have taken myself from a social media manager and student to a social media influencer, entrepreneur, marketing thought-leader, executive consultant, and women's empowerment advocate. The opportunities I've had might seem out of the ordinary, and you may be thinking, *She must be special*, or, *She is really lucky*. But they all resulted from building, focusing, and maintaining my personal brand to achieve my personal brand mission. This transformation and growth took place within a few years and required a lot of focus, but if I can do it, you can, too . . . and you will.

Repeat after me: Personal branding is for everyone, not just the privileged and well networked. When people write blogs and articles about how personal branding isn't a necessary or worthy act, they are actually building their brand—a brand based on eschewing personal branding. To reiterate, personal branding is for *everyone*, including you. Is it hard? No. Does it require effort and a strong work ethic? Yes. Half of the work is to consistently show up and be ready and available for the opportunities that arise.

Having a personal brand is inescapable. If you don't build and manage your brand, the world around you will do it for you, and you will be putting your future in the hands of others. This is risky. If you're trying to achieve greater success in your career, it is nonsensical to allow others to build your personal brand. Everything we do, everyone we associate with, every company we work for affects the way the world perceives us. To structure and maintain our reputations, we must develop and manage our own personal brands. This is not just a must-win for our careers. As artificial intelligence grows, we will start to see that our online presence, which is the most public expression of our personal brand, will be used in ways that affect our lives overall—to assess our risk for loans or our suitability for admission to educational institutions, for example. You are more than what you post: your audience's *perception* of you is your reality. Change their perception, and you create a new reality.

What does it take to develop and manage your own brand? You must create a strategy. Approach your personal brand with the same seriousness and due diligence that branding agencies show their corporate clients. In addition to your brand message, you need an audit, a goal-setting game plan, growth strategies, and an awareness of the space you are in or want to enter.

The goal is to define and demonstrate your identity in a way that accurately represents your successes and paints you as the person you want to be (not necessarily who you currently are). Your brand should bring you opportunity, not take it away from you. If your brand positively speaks on your behalf, then you get to remain modest in conversation. You should have a personal brand message that is immediately clear; your brand message both controls and dictates what people say about you when you are not in the room.

Take a look at some of the most well-known and studied personal brands in history: We have the Rockefellers (not recent but still relevant), Donald Trump, Kim Kardashian, Gary Vaynerchuk, Mark Cuban, Oprah Winfrey, and Martha Stewart, to name a few. We know these people really well. We have watched most of them go through some sort of public scrutiny at one time or another. We have also seen them quickly achieve the unthinkable. Kim Kardashian went from a leaked-sex-tape victim to *TIME* magazine's "Top 100 Most Influential People in 2015." Donald Trump transitioned from businessman to reality TV star to president of the United States.

Personal branding is built on four main factors: personal proof, social proof, recognition, and association. These are the elements that support your personal brand. However, you cannot successfully achieve any of these objectives without clear direction, planning, and goals. *Platform* will teach you my methodology for accelerated brand development, continuous brand management, growth and pivot strategies, and monetization.

You will learn how to build your own brand to achieve your goals and reach new heights in your career, all while having fun along the way. You will come to understand what it means to build a brand and how to get out of your own way so you can do this. Start with the realization that everything we think we know could possibly be wrong. This will help you gain the confidence to challenge the status quo and acquire the tools to make a splash in your industry and your life overall.

As you read *Platform*, keep in mind that personal branding is not a new concept but a tool that has been used by the privileged few who were willing to embrace it long before the rest of us. Today, personal branding is something we all need to do. By building my own brand and helping others build theirs, I have learned that there are significant benefits to cultivating your own public persona. If you define your direction, you will move quickly into positions of influence simply by controlling your own world and the elements surrounding it. Branding is technical, creative, spiritual, and scientific, and it is much easier than you think.

1 THE CASE FOR PERSONAL BRANDING

Many people believe that personal branding is a negative or selfish thing to do. There is a misconception that personal branding is about branding, packaging, and selling. This is not what personal branding is at all. Personal branding is self-awareness and self-preservation. I think of it as credit. You are not your credit score, but when you go to buy a house, your credit score will have a huge impact on your chances of being approved for a loan and what sort of interest you will pay. Your credit only matters when it comes into question for certain approvals.

Just as with credit, your personal brand comes into question only when someone is trying to approve your participation in something (a job, an event, or the like). And as with credit, having *no* personal brand can be just as damaging as having a bad one. The difference between your personal brand and your credit score is that you know when someone is looking to validate your credit score and you probably already know what they are expecting and going to see. With personal brands, most people have no idea when someone is looking for them online, what they hope to see, or what they will find. We give more attention to our credit scores than to our reputations.

Improve your personal brand the way you would improve your credit score. Personal branding is not just a promotional tool, it is the platform you stand on in front of the world. You have to know what the world sees, just as you know what the banks and landlords see when they check your credit.

» Make sure your credit report is accurate and the information about you online is accurate.

» When you find flaws in your credit report, you pinpoint what needs to be fixed. Do the same for your personal brand. Do you have too much debt or not enough? Do you have too much experience in one thing and not enough in another? How does that impact your next life goal?

» Create a plan to fix your credit. Create a plan to fix your personal brand.

» Build a strong credit age. Build your brand through experience.

» As when you apply for a credit card, ask for help from people. Think of credit as the asking and debt as the favors you owe. You don't want to ask for too much from people, and you always want to return the favor.

» Just as you wouldn't apply for a credit card with bad credit, don't ask for favors for your personal brand that you haven't earned.

» Set up alerts for your credit. Set up alerts for your personal brand.

Personal branding is for everyone. You have it even when you don't. You have credit even when you don't. Everyone in the digital age needs to be aware of their personal brand. It is no longer a choice whether to have one; the choice is whether you manage yours.

THE HISTORY AND PURPOSE OF BRANDING

Brands want to be more human. Why? Because brands want to connect with more humans. Brands fight to create a voice because they don't naturally have one. People, on the other hand, do. We are the most natural brand. We connect with other people, we have a voice, and we are what brands strive to be and to connect with. Brands have always gotten so much recognition because brands have actively marketed themselves, and not all humans have. People are not trying to be brands; brands are trying to be people.

Let me explain by outlining the history of branding.

AD 500 to 1000: The word *brand* is derived from an ancient Norse word that means "to burn." The word refers to the practice by companies of burning their marks (brands) onto their products.

AD 1500: By the 1500s, the word *brand* refers to burning a mark into cattle and livestock to show ownership and to identify lost or stolen livestock. Each livestock owner develops a unique "logo" so they can easily identify their livestock within the herd.

1820s: The world sees an increase in the mass production and shipment of trade goods. The larger the batches, the harder it is to distinguish one batch from the next. So producers stamp their logos onto the crates in which the products are shipped to demarcate their property from that of the competition.

1870: It becomes possible to register a trademark so that a company can prevent other businesses from using similar brands and logos to confuse consumers as customers discern one competitor's products from another's.

Early 1900s: Brands themselves become valuable. Brands start being associated with ideas and emotions. People begin buying brands that represent what they believe in. Advertisements show the benefits of brands.

1980s: Brand recognition becomes the most important focus for corporations, as competition starts to skyrocket and distribution channels become global. Corporate branding begins to evolve into culture creating. We start to see advertising agencies turn into branding consultancies, and corporations start working directly with political groups, nonprofits, and celebrities.

Late 1990s to early 2000s: The rise of social media changes the way brands interact with consumers. Branding is now about communicating with brands directly, reviewing them, holding them accountable, and using a new kind of celebrity—the digital influencer.

Branding was once a simple and straightforward tool for companies to clearly identify one product from another. Over time, this tool has changed. Brands and logos are now used by people as ways of telling the world who they are, what they are, and who they wish they were. The irony is that while brands and logos were created and used to differentiate two similar things from each other, now they are used to relate two seemingly unique things to each other.

Brands connect us with each other and with a lifestyle. We use social media to talk to them and about them, we like them, we share them, and we use them as tools for self-expression—and with each share, we endorse them. We also hide behind them and let them tell our stories for us. We don't have companies' logos burned into our skin, but we do walk around with their logos on display. And every time we purchase a product from a brand, we are subscribing to their ideology and practices, whether intentionally or not.

Don't believe me? See how quickly you can choose your preferences in this list:

Mac or PC?

Marvel or DC?

Coke or Pepsi?

Nike or Converse?

Tylenol or Advil?

Whole Foods or Trader Joe's?

Uber or Lyft?

Rotten Tomatoes or IMDb.com?

I'll bet you answered most of the questions in less than a second. How incredible is that? In each case, we have two companies offering the same service or product, yet we are able to choose between them within seconds. Mac and PC both offer computers; Nike and Converse both keep your feet protected; Rotten Tomatoes and IMDb are both websites that let you read reviews of movies written by other people. Why are we so quick to choose one over the other?

Because we want the world to know where we belong. We choose between computers to show that we are savvy and independent, or trendy. We choose between types of shoes because we want people to know that we are athletic or that we frequent concerts. We choose where to read our reviews because we want to trust the reviewers, and if they aren't like us, well, how can we trust their opinions? So we find the website that speaks to the person we want to be and the people we want to be like.

Sure, we could say that we shop at Trader Joe's because Whole Foods is more expensive. That is practical. Then again, many Trader Joe's shoppers also choose an iPhone over an Android. If cost is the deciding factor, then an iPhone is impractical. In theory, it makes little sense that someone would avoid shopping at Whole Foods to save money when they also purchase an iPhone over an Android. In reality, we see this all the time.

A few years ago, people were boycotting a fast-food chicken restaurant because the CEO made antihomosexual statements in an interview. In response to the boycott, the opposing side (the people who agreed with the antihomosexual statements) decided to rally across the United States to all eat at that restaurant on the same day. Social media went crazy with posts of people eating chicken at that chain restaurant. Many of the pictures were taken with iPhones, but the CEO of Apple, Tim Cook, is an openly homosexual man. In theory, it makes no sense that people would rally to support an antihomosexual CEO's brand while also supporting a brand with a homosexual CEO. In reality, it happens.

WHY CONTRADICTION AND CHAOS ARE A NECESSARY PART OF BRANDING

People identify brands with other people, and just like people, brands are judged based on the best and worst things they have ever done in the eyes and perspective of the person judging. People who do not believe in a homosexual lifestyle can overlook using an iPhone, because hiring a homosexual is not as damning to them as the Apple products are useful. And of course, Steve Jobs, not Tim Cook, still represents Apple in the eyes of most consumers. On the other hand, those who believe in the rights of homosexual people may boycott a restaurant because the food is not good, not because the CEO makes bigoted statements.

Contradictions stem from the ways we naturally trust people for certain observed behaviors and traits, both negative and positive. For instance, let's say you were a smoker and a slightly overweight person who quit smoking for your health and started working out. Then you hired a super-fit personal trainer who smoked after your workouts. You would naturally question whether smoking was really that bad for you or whether your trainer was the right person to work out with.

The other cause of contradictions in brand advocacy is assumption and natural association. When people are young and career driven, others might associate them with early rising, robotic tendencies, or an Ivy League education. If they don't fit that mold, they run the risk of upsetting the people who have made assumptions about their personalities. But they also benefit by gaining the attention of people who see them as unique, so they can engage a separate audience that will now find them more relatable.

Think about it this way: Should people who have never attended college speak at an Ivy League college's graduation? The answer: Only if they are more successful than the degree is valuable in the eyes of the students. Anything can happen if your greatest achievement is greater than the situation. This is how contradictory ideas, products, and people can coexist. If you want to speak at a Harvard graduation, you can do one of two things: go to college at Harvard and become more important than your degree or become more notable than a degree from Harvard.

WHY NOT YOU?

In his speech at Rice University in 1962, John F. Kennedy announced that the United States would be sending people to the moon. The first man landed on the moon on July 20, 1969. Ever since President Kennedy delivered his speech, twelve people have walked on the moon (most notably Neil Armstrong).

Whenever I hear, "That is just the way it has always been," I hear an excuse rather than a viable explanation. This type of thinking represents the acceptance of the unknown as forever unknown, and it can lead to an unquestioning belief and trust in those whom we appoint as leaders. There is nothing in this world that exists as it has always been. There is always a beginning, everything requires evolution (change), and in most cases there is an end (or simply another evolution). So if everything is constantly changing and evolving, why do we become complacent and accept things as they are in the present? Acceptance of the way things are stops us from asking "Why?" and "why not?" It stops us from seeking change and challenging ourselves to grow.

From a very young age, people are taught to obey rules and follow instructions. We are programmed to fit into the world as it exists and told to do our best within a structure that was created before us, which is often presented as if it were created *for* us. We are told directly and indirectly that many of the rules in life are set and that our main goal is to live and prosper according to these predetermined guidelines. In many instances, our metrics for success are also predetermined. We are taught to find a job, start a family, build a life, and obey the law. The majority of us will follow this path and build our lives within this construct because, well, that's the way it is and the way it has always been.

What about the people who do not follow these rules—the people who ask the world and themselves the difficult questions, who break away from the norm and see the potential for a life beyond pre-set limitations? These are the people who get to make new rules, remove old ones, and create a legacy. They are the ones, like Neil Armstrong, who are willing to take a leap of faith and believe in a world that differs from the one we see now, and who believe in themselves enough to take the first step. We remember these people because they help us challenge the criterion and they propel us forward to discover the unknown on our own. These people achieve personal autonomy, freedom of thought, and the euphoria that comes with freedom of expression. They are able to release themselves from the control of external influences and achieve a self-directed freedom that most of us don't even dare to dream of.

There is a scene in the film *The Matrix* in which Neo and Trinity are preparing to save Morpheus from the Smiths. Trinity looks at Neo and says, "No one has ever done this before," and Neo responds, "That's why it will work." That line has stuck with me since I was a kid, when I used to watch the film on repeat. I love that almost every scene requires a character to make a choice. In my mind, this is reality amplified.

HOW WE DIFFER FROM BRANDS

We are different from brands because we don't need people to wear our names or put our faces on their belongings. But we do have followers, connections, images with tags, groups, clubs, co-workers, personal connections, and more. When we connect with people online or offline, we are telling the world that we subscribe to them and that they subscribe to us. We are saying that we have something in common or share beliefs. The stronger and clearer your personal goals and ideals are defined online, the more the people who may not know you in person are inclined to subscribe to your personal brand.

Personal branding is not about packaging yourself to sell yourself. It is about bringing focus to your actions so that the right kinds of people can find you and subscribe to your message, and vice versa. Brands want to be people. They strive to evoke the same emotional connections that people create naturally. So you have a head start in that you already have a brand, and you have ownership over yourself. When you think about it from this perspective, "personal brand" is a misnomer; the words "personal autonomy" are more accurate. That said, the world has come to use personal brand to describe the result, and we will, too.

Personal branding starts with the ability to think for yourself as you make choices about what you buy, do, and represent because you like what you're choosing, not because you need to make those choices. Brands need people to help define their message, create a culture around their products, and carry their messages forward. Personal branding is about being yourself out loud. When we are truly ourselves, we contradict the norms, confuse people, intrigue them, and shift their thinking by shifting their perspectives.

We are different from brands because we are relatable. If you want to be heard, you need to understand why people will listen. You have to understand your own value proposition. You can change and sway it over time, but initially you have to understand what it is about you that will open doors. You also need to understand which rooms you should be in and which rooms are out of your league. Personal branding takes time, just as anything that really matters should.

Listen to your natural instincts and desires. Don't adapt or mold yourself to be the "next" anyone. Unlike brands that are desperately trying to become more like people and copying trends to do so, you are already a person; your brand should focus on being authentic instead of a manufactured version of what you think everyone else wants you to be.

PUBLIC RELATIONS IS PROPAGANDA IS PR IS NEWS

Propaganda is defined as information that is not objective and is used primarily to influence an audience and further an agenda. Edward Bernays was a twentieth-century journalist, author, and philosopher who is considered to be the father of propaganda. (Bernays renamed *propaganda* as "public relations" to sidestep the negative connotations associated with the word following World War II.) Bernays handled public relations for many noteworthy clients, including President Calvin Coolidge, Procter & Gamble, CBS, General Electric, Dodge Brothers Motor Car Company (as it was named at the time), and, most famously, the American Tobacco Company.

In the 1920s, while working for the American Tobacco Company, Bernays told the press that women's rights marchers would be attending the Easter Sunday Parade in New York City and lighting "torches of freedom." Bernays knew that by sending attractive women to a march with cigarettes, he would reframe the idea of women's smoking (it was taboo back then), freeing more women to smoke as an expression of their freedom and, consequently, radically increasing the market for cigarettes.

Instead of finding a group of women's rights activists, the media saw models (gathered by Bernays on behalf of the American Tobacco Company) marching in the parade and lighting up Lucky Strike cigarettes. The media didn't know the difference, and on April 1, 1929, the *New York Times* published images of the models under the headline "Group of Girls Puff at Cigarettes as a Gesture of Freedom." The event and the headline helped break the taboo against women smokers and smoking in public.

From this point forward, Bernays went on to craft many successful campaigns, to become the author of numerous books, and even to influence other infamous public relations professionals such as Ivy Lee, publicist to the Rockefellers.

Bernays was not just a publicist; he was also a philosopher and a nephew of famous neurologist Sigmund Freud. So it is no surprise that Bernays combined theories of crowd psychology with his uncle's psychoanalytical ideas to create an unstoppable concept of his own: public relations. You may be asking yourself what this has to do with personal branding. Well, this has everything to do with personal branding.

Bernays did not just take on a project and consider, *How can I sell this for my client?* He knew that selling something with the potential for great impact, whether an idea or a product, requires more than just a message. It requires a complete understanding of the buyer. You need to know what your buyers think about your commodity, how they think about it, whom they trust to learn it from, and what they are passionate about foremost. If you want to be influential, successful, and thought of as a leader, the first step is realizing that you have to think *for* yourself, not *about* yourself, in this process. The key to influence is realizing that it is not about you; it is about the people you are influencing and how the message affects them.

For example, no one cares that you think you are the next Steve Jobs. In fact, no one cares if you actually *are* the next Steve Jobs, until they hear it from someone else. This is the power of third-party authorities—or as you know them today, influencers, thought leaders, executives, corporations, and, of course, the media. If *TIME* publishes an article that declares you "the next Steve Jobs," then people will start to believe that you may in fact be the new innovator of your day.

The idea of using third-party authorities is not new. In fact, Bernays used this method often and as early as the start of the 1900s. Bernays wrote his theory in his 1928 book, *Propaganda*. He is quoted as saying, "If you can influence the leaders, either with or without their conscious cooperation, you automatically influence the group which they sway." So if the business publication *Bloomberg* can sway the opinion of the people who purchase stocks, then there is no need for you to go after everyone who buys stocks. Instead, sway the opinion of *Bloomberg*, and everyone else will follow.

Branding is about making brands more human, and personal branding is about making humans more authentic. Personal branding is about personal autonomy, personal growth, and individual thought. It is about being more human, not more brand-like. Brands have always strived to be more human, because the more human a brand is, the more people identify with it. When it comes to personal branding, however, it isn't so much about being more human as it is about strategically accessing an audience. That is why influencers can charge brands so much for their support: the brands need them. People want the opinions of those they trust. The way to build trust with other people is effective communication. Fortunately for us, today we have plenty of resources we can use to create conversation and demonstrate trust. That has not always been the case. There was a time when word of mouth, printed news, and snail mail were the only tools we had available for reputation management and personal branding. Of course, those tools were mainly utilized by the elite.

THE ROCKEFELLERS: ONE OF THE WORLD'S FIRST PERSONAL BRANDS

Ivy Lee, the second-most-infamous person in public relations, was greatly influenced by Edward Bernays and was the publicist to the Rockefeller family and Standard Oil. He also happened to be the uncle of the famous novelist William S. Burroughs (who wrote *Naked*

Lunch). Lee was hired by John D. Rockefeller Jr. to represent his family and Standard Oil after a coal mining rebellion in Colorado, known as the Ludlow Massacre.

To understand the need for Ivy Lee and personal branding, it is important that you understand the Ludlow Massacre and how the Rockefellers were associated with it. In the late 1800s and early 1900s, railway trains were popping up all over the United States, and they needed coal to operate. This of course made coal a valued commodity of the time. In the early 1900s, Colorado was home to the largest coal operator in the West, Colorado Fuel and Iron Company, purchased by John D. Rockefeller in 1902 and given to his son, John D. Rockefeller Jr., in 1911. John D. Jr. lived in New York City and managed the operation from his office on Broadway.

As we know today, coal mining is extremely dangerous, and in 1912 the labor laws were effectively nonexistent. Miners in Colorado were not paid by the day or by the hour but by how much coal they produced, which naturally led to being overworked in dangerous conditions just to put food on the table.

When welfare capitalism—the idea that coal-mine owners could subsidize the cost of living for their miners by essentially owning the towns they lived in—entered the scene, it meant better health care, homes, and education for miners' families. But then the miners' lives became almost completely controlled by their employers, with little opportunity to escape once they grew accustomed to the lifestyle. These days we call that scenario a company town—or, dare I say, Googletown? But in 1912 Colorado coal-mining towns, the company towns were not run by Google. The towns imposed rules on the personal lives of the miners, in the same way they did while the miners were at work. This meant curfews enforced, no strange guests allowed, and guards with guns on patrol to make sure everyone obeyed. The coal miners were understandably frustrated by these working conditions, so they started to unionize nationally. The unions wanted labor laws, better working conditions, and fewer work-related deaths. The Western Federation of Miners, the union responsible for unionizing the western states, decided to focus attention on Colorado first, starting with none other than the Rockefeller-owned Colorado Fuel and Iron Company. The coal company's response and plan to stop the progress of unionization was to hire strikebreakers to work for a lower wage in place of the striking workers. The strikebreakers were mostly from Mexico and Eastern Europe.

The strike took place in 1913, and the union presented the Colorado Fuel and Iron Company with the following list of demands on behalf of the miners:

» To recognize the union as a bargaining agent for the mine workers

» To pay miners for digging every two thousand pounds of coal, not every twenty-two hundred pounds

» To enforce the eight-hour workday law

» To pay miners for the work that did not result in producing coal but aided in the process, such as laying track and cutting wood

» To hold a workers' vote to select the weight-check men who kept track of the weight of the coal to be billed (like managers) and to remove those who were dishonest

» To give miners the right to choose any store, doctor, education, and home they wanted

» To enforce the laws of the state of Colorado, such as work-safety rules, and to remove the guards

This all seems pretty fair, right? Well, the company refused to comply with the union's demands, and the workers went on strike. Men who went on strike were immediately removed from their homes (along with their families) and went to live in tents on land leased by the union. The company hired more strikebreakers and a private detective agency to protect the working miners from the strikers and to harass the strikers. Yes, this really happened; just think for a minute how much has changed when you consider that "chief happiness officer" is an official job at some of the most influential companies today.

On April 20, 1914, the guards from the mines came to the union camps and demanded the release of a man they believed was being held by the union against his will. The union denied the accusation, and the guards (mixed with men from the detective agency in guard uniforms) opened fire on the union tents. Trains came by and picked up some of the families to move them to safety, but many did not make it. Along the tracks lay the bodies of more than a dozen men who had died in the attack. Fire was set to a tent where eleven children and four women were sheltering, taking the lives of all eleven children and two of the women. The leader of the union was found shot in the head, his body dumped beside the railroad tracks in full view of the passing trains. It remained there for three days before a local demanded that the body be moved for burial.

The Ludlow Massacre left twenty-four people dead. John D. Rockefeller Jr. and the Rockefeller family were widely criticized for this event. Under the guidance of their publicist, Ivy Lee, the Rockefellers started a campaign that became the first of its kind. Lee sent the Rockefellers to Colorado to meet with the coal miners, listen to family members, host events in their honor, and inspect their working and living conditions. It was a campaign that would humanize the Rockefeller family in order to repair their damaged reputation and ultimately save their businesses. The idea that the people being held responsible for such a massacre would face the families of the deceased was unheard-of and drew a lot of media attention. Lee pushed the Rockefellers to create the Rockefeller Center in New York City and put their name on the building. He understood that one of the primary reasons it was easy for the public to blame the Rockefellers was because they were known for being wealthy and nothing else.

Humanizing the Rockefellers made them relatable to the masses. It is easier for people to hate a business than to hate and publicly attack a fellow human being. How does this work? Because your personal brand is not about you: it is 100 percent based on others' opinions of you. If you are a billionaire who sits in an ivory tower and never comes down to say hello, then you are probably seen as a greedy jerk. If you are a billionaire who speaks directly with people, owns your success, and tells others that you believe they can find similar success, then you will be relatable (and, as it turns out, you can even become the president of the United States of America). The more time you spend communicating with your audience and relating to them, the better they will think of you and everything you are associated with thereafter.

Here's another way to think of it. Have you ever heard a story about someone who met a celebrity or famous person? They say either, "He/she was lovely," or "They were so rude; they must be full of themselves." The difference in the opinion is all in the communication. If the person stops to say hello or acknowledges you, then they are lovely. If they rush past you for any reason (and we all have our reasons), then they are rude. Communication is key, and no communication at all is as much a choice as overcommunication.

The Rockefellers were able to win the hearts of people whose loved ones had died as a result of the company's poor business practices, simply by showing up and listening. But that is not enough for personal branding today. If you are able to build an audience and a recognizable brand, you will then have to put in the work to manage it.

HATERS DON'T REALLY HATE, THEY JUST DON'T UNDERSTAND

Many people, media outlets, and even some educators have been painting a picture of personal branding as a self-interested, millennial-created phenomena. Not true. Yet some thought-leaders, such as

Facebook's chief operating officer and author of *Lean In*, Sheryl Sandberg, have come out against building personal brands.

I like what Sheryl Sandberg has to say on many other topics. I think she is honest and intelligent, hard-working, and a great role model for women and men everywhere. She genuinely wants to help inform and is truly a person to look up to if you want a career similar to hers. But I disagree with her completely on the topic of personal branding. First, brands are not products; brands are symbols for what the products represent. Brands are created by businesses to represent the value the companies are trying to bring to the market. Second, personal branding is not about packaging an inauthentic version of yourself. It is claiming your voice and becoming more authentic by removing the logos, imprints, stereotypes, and perceptions to take control of your own images, reputations, and freedom of thought. Third, what we don't say can be as telling as what we do say and how, where, when we say it, making personal branding about more than simply having a voice.

Sandberg's view of personal branding is understandable—she may not be aware she has a personal brand because hers was built almost circumstantially, not out of necessity (though she has done a great job maintaining it). Sandberg joined Google in 2001 (Google was founded in 1998). She joined Facebook in 2008. (Facebook was founded in 2004 but was limited to college students, until it became available to anyone over the age of thirteen in 2006.) Fast-forward a decade, and we live in an era where everyone is online, everyone expects you to be online, and people will search for you long before they will ever accept a meeting with you. Sandberg has helped get us here by leading the top information, communication, and media-distribution tools that have made personal branding not just a reality but a requirement.

Put yourself in the shoes of people who enter the job market after years of posting on Facebook, who have their LinkedIn profiles viewed before they're ever asked for a résumé, who re-enter the job market after losing a job in the career they've had for decades, or who are returning to the workforce after having children and have no online presence as they search for a new job. It's not just an advantage to develop your personal brand; it's a distinct disadvantage if you don't.

REALLY LISTEN

In the early 1980s, the world found itself in the midst of a health epidemic with the discovery of HIV and AIDS. The disease was first observed and reported by the media within the male homosexual community in Los Angeles and New York City. We knew little about the disease at the time, other than that it was extremely contagious and was rapidly spreading within the male homosexual population.

For years, it was believed that touching someone who had the AIDS virus without protection would put you at risk for contracting HIV. People with HIV and AIDS were quarantined in dedicated hospital units and interacted only with doctors who were in full protective gear. Those suffering from the disease and the entire homosexual community were faced with a stigma that stemmed from the fear of not knowing. Then something incredible happened.

In April 1997, Diana, Princess of Wales, walked through the newly opened AIDS ward at Middlesex Hospital in London with the media in tow and shook hands with an HIV-positive man without wearing a glove. At the time, the patient did not want to be named or photographed because of the public's perception of the disease, so the photographer took the picture with the patient's back facing the camera. With this single gesture of kindness, Princess Diana told the world that compassion and understanding for people affected by this disease were more important than fear and ignorance. She unexpectedly changed the future of HIV and AIDS research, awareness, and the stigma associated with it.

Princess Diana did not have to take an interest in this cause or the suffering of this community. Instead of following royal guidelines and maintaining her royal distance, she thought for herself about the well-being of others. She challenged the status quo—not only for herself but for people all over the world.

So many people think that personal branding is for those who want power and influence, but it is really for people who want freedom from being influenced or overpowered by others.

In a recent study on power from the University of Cologne, the University of Groningen, and Columbia University, each institution presented two different concepts of power—power as influence and power as autonomy. "Power as influence is expressed in having control over others, which could involve responsibility for others," the researchers wrote. "In contrast, power as autonomy is a form of power that allows one person to ignore and resist the influence of others and thus to shape one's own destiny."[1]

Princess Diana knew the power she possessed and understood her reputation, so she knew exactly what message she would send when she shook hands with a man who was HIV positive. She knew because she was really listening to the patients and understood at a deep level what a handshake would mean to that man as well as how it could help many people in the world overcome their fears. She took control of the situation, and in turn, she took control of her brand and the way the world perceived her and HIV patients.

LISTEN MORE THAN YOU SPEAK

Even smart, well-informed people can be misinformed or send the wrong message by being misunderstood. I prefer to research the reasoning behind positions and practices myself.

We often hear experts cited who have finished studying or have retired, sometimes many years earlier, yet they are still considered experts. Shouldn't it be a requirement to stay relevant if you want to remain an expert at something? Are they really experts now, or are they more like historians?

The more I learn about some of the most common things in our society, the more I realize how many opportunities there are for change and how much room there is to create it. This discovery has influenced my own personal branding as well as the advice I give my clients. The more we learn about things that are widely accepted but aren't true or don't make sense, the more it reinforces the little voice in our heads that says, *Why doesn't anyone listen to me?* If no one is thinking for themselves, then who is doing the thinking? *You* can do the thinking, and that is what informs your brand. Here are a few examples that underscore this.

Case One: Two Pennies to Rub Together

In 2014, a single penny cost 1.7 cents to manufacture.[2] That means it cost 1.7 times the value of a penny to mint one (the commodity metal value plus the cost to mint). That same year, it cost the United States government (US taxpayers) 8.1 cents for every nickel that was minted, according to the United States Mint. That means that five pennies cost more to make than one nickel. Don't take my word for it, do the math: 1.7 x 5 = 8.5 cents, compared to the nickel that cost 8.1 cents in 2014.

What's the best part of all of this? US pennies were the most-produced coin in 2014, representing 61.3 percent of the year's production total. There were 8.1 billion pennies produced in 2014, which is worth $81 million in pennies. The grand total spent to make pennies in 2014 was approximately $137.7 million. That is $137 million to produce $100 million in pennies. Yet we leave pennies all over the ground, in those little trays near the registers at convenience stores, and in fountains throughout the country. Our parking meters won't even accept pennies. Americans pay taxes to produce a coin that we lose money on, and then we leave that money on the ground and even throw it in the trash.

Additionally, in 2016 the United States Mint produced 9.16 billion pennies. Yes, in 2016 the penny cost only 1.5 cents to make (down from 2014), but we aren't saving any money. The Mint does make money on the production of dimes and quarters, but we produce significantly fewer of them than pennies. (In 2015, the Mint produced only 2.87 billion dimes and 2.65 billion quarters.)

So why are we still using pennies? The argument for keeping them is that we need them for rounding off prices, so people can sell things for ninety-nine cents. Businesses would lose money if they rounded prices down to ninety-five cents, and consumers would end up spending more if retailers rounded up prices to a dollar. But we already leave our pennies everywhere, and we are paying more to make pennies than they are worth. Who would mind if we paid a penny more?

Case Two: The Value of Anything Is the Value You Give It

When I was about seven years old, I stood on the side of the street outside my aunt's house with my sister, who was only three or four. I collected a bunch of rocks, painted faces on them, and had my sister ask passersby if they wanted to buy a rock. Many people laughed, and some gave us money but left the rock. I got in trouble for making my little sister sell rocks to strangers. I understand why my mom was angry. It took me awhile to understand why potential buyers laughed at us, but I accepted that our idea was a dumb one and moved on.

It wasn't until I was in my twenties that I realized I may have been onto something. That was the day I heard about a man named Gary Dahl, a creative person who owned an advertising agency in California. In 1975, Gary Dahl got tired of hearing his friends complain about their pets, so he invented the Pet Rock.[3] He wrote an instructional manual on how to take care of a Pet Rock, packaged it nicely, and sold 1.5 million of them for four dollars each that year. His profit? Three dollars per Pet Rock, quickly making him a millionaire for selling rocks.

Let's look at the value of our labor. If you were told today that a rock could sell for more than you make in an hour or even in a day at your job, would that surprise you? Well, in December 2016, Nordstrom's put rocks on sale.[4] They had two versions of the rock wrapped in leather pouches—a small one for sixty-five dollars and a larger one for eighty-five dollars. Both rocks sold out on their website. The online description of the leather-wrapped rocks read: "A paperweight? A conversation piece? A work of art? It's up to you." At least Gary Dahl had told us what the rock was used for: his rocks were pets. The overpriced Nordstrom's rocks left the use of the rock for buyers to determine. Think about this the next time you're pricing your labor and messaging your value.

If rocks can make people millionaires and sell out in 2016—when they were more expensive than a tank of gas—then anything is possible.

Case Three: Does an Apple a Day Keep the Doctor Away?

I was in Dubai as a guest at the World Government Summit. The huge event was packed with industry and world leaders, and we could attend a variety of functions each night. One of the options I attended was the Gourmet Waste dinner, with ambassadors, executives, and people from the local government. We were there to eat food that had almost gone bad but had not yet spoiled. This was a difficult dinner for me, because I am not a foodie and have difficulty stomaching food that I know might be spoiled. To be fair, the food was fine. It was my preconceived notion of what I was eating that was the problem. I was afraid that I wouldn't be able to finish my dinner at an event about not wasting food.

Then the United Arab Emirates (UAE) Minister of Climate Change and Environment, Dr. Thani Ahmed Al Zeyoudi, stood up and introduced the chef and the scientist in attendance. The scientist asked us how long we thought it would take for the average apple to arrive on the grocery store shelf after it had been picked. We all threw out random guesses. We were all wrong. "Nearly a year," he answered, adding that by the time a store-bought apple reaches our homes, much of the nutrition is gone, depending on how long it was stored.

What the scientist said is true: apples can take up to a year to get to your local grocery store.[5] Depending on where you get your apples, how you eat them, and what you eat them with, they may not actually keep the doctor away. (Is anyone else a little annoyed with their mom after reading this?)

What am I getting at here? In a world where pennies cost more to make than they are worth, retailers are selling rocks and making a killing, and apples are less healthful than we've been told, anything is possible. When we think beyond what we think we know, we need experimental thinking—individual thinking. We need to question our experts and be fearless in challenging the norms that keep everyone moving in the same direction. When you think for yourself, your ideas become the base value of your brand.

2 DEFINE YOUR OWN METRICS FOR SUCCESS

What do you want to do? For most of us, even that one question can be daunting. Some of us want to do a million different things, and some of us have no idea what we want to do, but most of us know what we *don't* want to do. Which is why I always encourage people to start with acknowledging what they don't want to do. If you can remove the things you don't want in your life, you will begin making room to test out new things that you might want. To start eliminating what you don't want, first you will have to recognize what those things are. Not only do you have to think for yourself but you also have to be honest with yourself. It can be as simple as not wanting to drive more than five miles to work or as complex as not wanting to continue in a career that you have spent a lot of time and money to build.

If you want to stand out, you have to be unabashedly your most authentic self and passionate about something to the point of obsession. You have to know what you care about and don't care about to know who you are. In an ideal world, you would know the answer to all three of those questions, but in a realistic world you have to start where you are. Again, many of us know only what we don't want, and that's okay. Having clarity about what you don't want and knowing that you aren't sure what you do want doesn't make you less authentic. Admitting it makes you more authentic.

Trying to figure out who you are and what you want can be frustrating; it is difficult to be objective about yourself. That's one reason actors and other people in the entertainment industry have agents and managers (also because agents negotiate contracts more effectively). These professionals help creatives see what they are, what they are not, and what they could be. Mr. (Fred) Rogers was the king of authenticity, who had a magical way of making us feel comfortable in our own skin. It was he who said, "Discovering the truth about ourselves is a lifetime's work, but it is worth the effort."

EVERYTHING THAT I KNEW WAS NOT FOR ME

I did not know what I wanted in my career and life. I was not one of those people who "just knew." But I did know what I didn't want and could recognize it quickly in a new situation. I didn't want to be told what to do or how to do it by anyone chosen at random. I had a difficult time respecting people whom I perceived as out of their elements. I didn't want to have to be on the phone all day long. I didn't want a job that required me to be in an office, in a chair, all day long. I didn't want a job that limited my travel experiences, and this helped me to realize that I wanted a job that allowed or required me to travel. I never wanted to hear the words, "Ask human resources."

As I was collecting my list of things that I didn't want, I had no idea what all of it meant for my direction or career. I just kept trying new things until I found something else that didn't make me happy, and then I would move on. I always felt that my happiness was dependent on avoiding things that made me unhappy. I believe that all of the little sacrifices and exceptions we make in our lives have a negative effect on us in the long run. So I trained myself to identify the feeling that something wasn't right and to quit soon after I recognized it.

My own life is my work, and the jobs that I take on are merely tasks in my life. If you got through a task that you hated, you would do whatever you could to never go back to it, right? I definitely wouldn't sacrifice forty-plus hours per week, fifty weeks per year, for my entire life. Don't get me wrong—I understand about paying dues. But I also think that you can easily recognize what won't change right after you have done the work. If you want to be a lawyer, you will always have to read, write, and work cases. If you want to be a doctor, you will always have to see patients.

While you're doing the work to take you to the next thing, you might not know what is a forever thing and what isn't. What I did was start a list and add to it everything new that wasn't for me. Whenever I started a new position, I would study the lifestyle of the person in charge, knowing that you get more autonomy as you grow in a company. If I noticed that they were forced to do things that I would never want to do, it was a sign that the job probably wasn't a good fit for me. Then I took my list of "don't wants" and flipped it to define what I did want.

SAYING "NO" TO ONE THING CREATES ROOM IN YOUR LIFE FOR SOMETHING ELSE

I used to define what I wanted in life as *freedom*—the freedom to do whatever it was that I wanted. When I first started my career, I believed (as many do) that films, photography, and art were about freedom. I wanted to work with the free thinkers, the people who told stories and influenced the world.

After high school, I decided to attend the Art Institute of Las Vegas to study film production. I took classes for two weeks and quickly realized not only that I could not draw but that I hated drawing. The first two semesters of my career at the Art Institute required that I learn to draw. I went to the school administration and asked if I could switch majors.

"To what?" they asked.

"Anything that doesn't require art classes—maybe interior design?" I replied.

The woman looked at me quizzically, as she had every right to do. "This is the Art Institute of Las Vegas. All of our degree programs require that you take art classes," she retorted.

When I heard that, I immediately replied, "Well, then, I quit." I added *drawing* to my list of things I didn't want.

At the time, I was the theater manager for a hypnotist at the Paris Hotel in Las Vegas at night and working part-time in marketing and promotions for local celebrities during the day. One day, it hit me: Why would I help promote these entertainers when I could just become one? I had years of acting, theater, and improv behind me, and this would give me the freedom I had always sought. I found a school, auditioned, got in, and within a couple of months I was on my way to Hollywood.

I studied stage choreography, theater, and phonetics. I completed the two-year program and started my career as an actress. Six months in, I quit and added *waiting* to the list of things I did not want in my life. I found that with acting and stunt choreography I had no control over my life or my time. I thought acting would bring me freedom, and instead I found out that I spent more time waiting around for something to happen than doing anything else. I would wait for auditions, for call-backs, on "holds" (the casting director gives you a bunch of days when they may or may not need you and asks you to be available for all of them), for the production team on the job, and then wait four to six weeks after the job to get paid. When I wasn't waiting for a new job in the acting world, I was waiting tables at the local Cheesecake Factory. I was quite literally a professional *waiter*.

This was just the beginning of my quitting experience. I went on to study anthropology and quit. I worked in a talent management office and quit. I ran marketing for a smoothie company and quit after three days. I worked accounts and receivables for a small record label and quit. The list goes on. All I ever knew was what I didn't want. I needed to quit all of these ventures in order to find my real passion.

When I was twenty-four, I was still in school studying business and Mandarin Chinese. I had taken a job as an intern for an internet company. The job was great, but I was focused on starting some sort of business in China at some point. So when they offered me a full-time job, I said, "No, thank you." A few months went by and my plans changed again; I decided that I was going to go backpacking for six months and think about where else in the world I may want to live someday. I had a mini–quarter-life crisis. I needed to know that there was more to life than what was right in front of me. I decided that I would sell everything I owned and leave the country. Even if I sold everything, including my car (which I did), I knew I would probably need more money. So to make money for my trip, I took the job that the internet company had offered me a few months earlier.

THINK FOR YOURSELF, NOT FOR OTHERS

A few weeks before I was going to leave for my trip, I called home and said, "Mom, I am quitting so I can travel the world." She was used to my frequent course corrections at this point, so instead of saying, "Are you crazy?" she said, "Don't quit. You will need a job when you get back." But what boss would let me leave for such a long time and hold my position for my return? I was an entry-level employee without a degree.

I walked into my boss's office and blurted, "I need to take some time off." He asked me how much time, and I replied, "Six, maybe nine months." He stared at me for a long time and then said, "I will be right back."

He was gone for maybe ten minutes, but it felt like forever. When he walked back in, he had a folder. He opened the folder, looked at me and said, "If you quit, we can't hire you back. That is company policy." I was ready to say good-bye.

But he continued, "Can you work five to ten hours per month?" Completely stunned, I said that I could. "Then we can give you a stipend to manage our social media posts while you are away," he said. "That way, you take a leave of absence, and then you can come back to work upon your return."

I was flabbergasted. I had just received everything I wanted that I wasn't even aware I wanted. My mom's advice was the most life-changing guidance I had ever received. Who would have known that I could get that much time off with pay and no explanation for why I needed to take the time off? In that moment, I realized I had been making assumptions about other people's thinking my whole life. If I was going to start thinking for myself, I needed to stop thinking for other people. When you ask before you assume, the opportunities are endless. I started asking for everything and anything I wanted. I didn't always get what I asked for, but here's a list of things I did receive:

» Free food, hotel, and tours in exchange for setting up Yelp and other online local listings for companies while I traveled

» An all-expenses-paid, six-week tour through New Zealand in exchange for a few tweets—I had a thousand followers at the time

» Seven months away from my job with paid leave of absence

» A free round-trip flight on a private jet in exchange for a tweet and a snap

» A 65 percent raise just nine months into the position, with no additional responsibilities

» A byline in a major publication when I had no prior editorial experience

» Sponsored suits, gowns, and alcohol at my pending nuptials

» Free facials, B12 shots, massages, and dental work in exchange for consulting

» Trips to Israel, Dubai, Mumbai, Manila, Hangzhou, Bali, and more, to speak at and attend events and retreats

» Computers, cash, and lots of wine

The list goes on. People love to barter. You can make room for endless possibilities if you simply give up control and ask for what you want, but this also requires acknowledging that what you have to offer in return is of value.

Why do we have such difficulty asking for what we want? It is how we are programmed from Day One. We fear being rejected so much that we would prefer to live without or go with less if it means that we can avoid hearing the word "No." This is a common and irrational fear. People like to do things for others. When we do a favor for someone else, our bodies get natural boosts from endorphins. Ask. If people say, "Yes," you have given an endorphin rush; if the response is "No," you will be no further ahead than when you started (and neither will anyone else). Ask, ask, and ask some more. We only become more successful and achieve goals with the help of others. If one person says no, ask another, or offer something new, but never stop asking for what you want or need.

PUT YOUR MASK ON FIRST

Every time we get on a plane to fly anywhere, we hear the instruction to secure our own masks before helping others in the event there's an emergency. Why is it important to place your mask on first? A man named Destin Sandlin, engineer and founder of popular podcast and YouTube channel *Smarter Every Day* had the same question.[6] He decided that he was going to find out why. In order to define the test, Destin needed to get to the bottom of what he was talking about: What are the effects of oxygen deprivation, or hypoxia?

Destin joined astronaut Don Pettit when Pettit went to renew his hypoxia training at NASA's Neutral Buoyancy Laboratory. The purpose of this training is to help astronauts and pilots understand the symptoms of hypoxia in order to identify when their brains have stopped working properly in the case of an emergency. The problem? No one experiences hypoxia the same way. So NASA had to find a way to train people about hypoxia in a way that allowed for the variations of the symptoms to be understood. The answer? Every person undergoing the training would have to experience the effects of hypoxia. So NASA put these people in a box that simulated the low-oxygen effect of high altitude and regulated the pressure of oxygen using the same kind of pressurization system that enables us to breathe on airplanes in a higher atmosphere.

For a trained astronaut, this experiment is nothing new. For a YouTube producer like Destin, this experiment is unique. The YouTube episode is filmed so that we can see the entire experiment as it progresses. The astronaut, Don, is considered the control, or the part of the experiment that gives results we are aware of and expect. He is familiar with his reaction to hypoxia, and he will put his mask back on as soon as he feels the symptoms. For Don, the symptoms are blurred tunnel vision and "air hunger," or the feeling of needing more air. Destin is given permission to keep his mask off for one minute beyond the point when the effects of hypoxia start to show. The results are fascinating.

Destin is given plastic pieces in various shapes as well as a bucket with the shapes cut out to fit the pieces into place. He goes on for about two minutes, announces the shapes accurately, and gets them all into the bucket using their appropriate holes. Then something strange happens. Destin starts smiling uncontrollably, he is slightly shaking, and his lips are turning purple. He is told that he needs to put his mask back on or he is going to die. Destin responds, "I don't want to die," but never puts his mask back on his face. The team inside the experiment has to put Destin's mask back on for him because he cannot comprehend how to do it at this point. Once his mask is back on, he is back to normal within seconds and can easily complete the new set of tasks.

What is the point of this story? We cannot help others to breathe if we aren't breathing ourselves. This is true for almost all elements of our lives. It is much easier to help others succeed if you are successful yourself. It is easier to make other people happy if you are happy yourself. And it is easier to make connections for others if you are well connected yourself. It is not selfish to think of your needs before you think of the needs of others. Entire communities of people are limited by their surroundings and networks simply because the culture of modesty and self-sacrifice inhibits them.

For example, we all know of one person who made a big break—the one who made it bigger than everyone else. This person ends up being the reason a community, family, or group of friends are now able to grow beyond their traditional means. How? They open access to a new way of living and a host of new opportunities that were not available before because of a lack of connections. These individuals had to be self-sufficient and successful before they could ever be of help to anyone else.

This is where personal branding comes in. It is about understanding that you must improve yourself before you can assist and bring meaning to someone else. Being influential is all about adding value to the lives of other people.

3 YOU ARE WHO YOU SAY YOU ARE

Personal branding also involves a lot of storytelling. I like to think of it as the evolution of the résumé—our own brief history of who we are. *Résumé* is a French word that means "summary" and directly translates into English as "abstract." Our résumés define not only what we have done but how we think. In today's world, the résumé is for everyone, not just job-seekers, and it is not limited to a sheet of paper. Your résumé is everywhere. We use résumés to decide whether we want to pick up people for ride-share services; we use them to determine whether we want to swipe right on someone's profile in a dating app or even whether we would invite them to dinner. The résumé has evolved into a sort of wiki for our lives.

Technology has evolved as well, and no one will wait for your résumé to decide whether they want to meet with you. No one is going to wait until they've met you on a first date before looking you up online. Today, even your grandparents communicate with you more frequently on Facebook than by telephone. We should all be aware that pretty much everything about us online is fair game for someone to make an assessment about our worthiness for new opportunities.

THE EVOLUTION OF THE RÉSUMÉ

Who wrote the first résumé? The first use of a résumé is credited to none other than the great Italian artist, architect, and engineer, Leonardo da Vinci. In 1481 or 1482 (the actual year is unknown), da Vinci wrote this handwritten résumé to the Duke of Milan:

> Most Illustrious Lord, Having now sufficiently considered the specimens of all those who proclaim themselves skilled contrivers of instruments of war, and that the invention and operation of the said instruments are nothing different from those in common use: I shall endeavor, without prejudice to anyone else, to explain myself to your Excellency, showing your Lordship my secret, and then offering them to your best pleasure and approbation to work with effect at opportune moments on all those things that, in part, shall be briefly noted below.

1. I have [plans for] a sort of extremely light and strong bridge, adapted to be most easily carried, and with them you may pursue, and at any time flee from the enemy; and others, secure and indestructible by fire and battle, easy and convenient to lift and place. Also, methods of burning and destroying those of the enemy.

2. I know how, when a place is besieged, to take the water out of the trenches, and make endless variety of bridges, and covered ways and ladders, and other machines pertaining to such expeditions.

3. If, by reason of the height of the banks, or the strength of the place and its position, it is impossible, when besieging a place, to avail oneself of the plan of bombardment, I have methods for destroying every rock or other fortress, even if it were founded on a rock, etc.

4. Again, I have kinds of mortars; most convenient and easy to carry; and with these I can fling small stones almost resembling a storm; and with the smoke of these cause great terror to the enemy, to his great detriment and confusion.

5. And if the fight should be at sea I have kinds of many machines most efficient for offense and defense; and vessels that will resist the attack of the largest guns and powder and fumes.

6. I have means by secret and tortuous mines and ways, made without noise, to reach a designated spot, even if it were needed to pass under a trench or a river.

7. I will make covered chariots, safe and unattackable, which, entering among the enemy with their artillery, there is no body of men so great but they would break them. And behind these, infantry could follow quite unhurt and without any hindrance.

8. In case of need I will make big guns, mortars, and light ordnance of fine and useful forms, out of the common type.

9. Where the operation of bombardment might fail, I would contrive catapults, mangonels, trabocchi, and other machines of marvellous efficacy and not in common use. And in short, according to the variety of cases, I can contrive various and endless means of offense and defense.

10. In times of peace I believe I can give perfect satisfaction and to the equal of any other in architecture and the composition of buildings public and private; and in guiding water from one place to another.

11. I can carry out sculpture in marble, bronze, or clay, and also, I can do in painting whatever may be done, as well as any other, be he who he may.

    Again, the bronze horse may be taken in hand, which is to be to the immortal glory and eternal honor of the prince your father of happy memory, and of the illustrious house of Sforza.

    And if any of the above-named things seem to anyone to be impossible or not feasible, I am most ready to make the experiment in your park, or in whatever place may please your Excellency—to whom I comment myself with the utmost humility, etc.

Da Vinci's résumé is the perfect kind of story that all résumés in the form of personal branding should tell. Today, you would strive to be less direct and use more signaling tactics, but that is the message.

Write a blog post about certain situations you face or your opinion on how to face them, and then post it on your LinkedIn. For instance, if you want to be a thought-leader in wealth management, identify a potential negative situation and write a post about what you would do if you were the one to solve it. Then, whenever people look at your LinkedIn profile or search for you online, they'll find that story—the story of you solving their potential problem.

Just as da Vinci did, make sure you keep a few personal notes in the brand mix. In *How Google Works*, coauthor Eric Schmidt discusses how he decides whether or not to hire someone, which *Fortune* magazine relays as, "Imagine being stuck at an airport with a colleague; Eric always chooses LAX for maximum discomfort (although Atlanta or London will do in a pinch). Would you be able to pass the time in a good conversation with him? Would it be time well spent, or would you quickly find yourself rummaging through your carry-on for your tablet so you can read your latest email or the news or anything to avoid having to talk to this dull person?"[7]

If your personal résumé, digital presence, and personal brand messaging are all business, you are going to be labeled "boring." No one wants to work with boring, and no one wants to hire boring to speak at their events. They want people who are qualified, ambitious, and know how to hold a conversation. Leonardo da Vinci knew this. He wrote a résumé that identified problems, provided solutions, and gave insight into his personality and hobbies. This is something to think about as you craft your personal brand story online. What are you saying to people? Does your personality shine through, or is it all business?

THE POST-DA VINCI RÉSUMÉ

Here we are today, 450 years after the first résumé was created. Following da Vinci's résumé, we don't see résumés in widespread use for another fifty years. In the 1930s, we can see the reemergence of the résumé (still handwritten) and how it slowly starts to pick up traction.

> **1940s:** Women are discouraged from writing résumés, and men are told that theirs should include a photo, marital status, age, social background, height, weight, and religion.

> **1950s:** Résumés become commonplace and are expected at every job interview.

> **1960s:** People add their personal interests such as hobbies, clubs, and sports to their résumés.

> **1970s:** Technology is moving forward, and people start typing their résumés instead of handwriting them.

> **1980s:** How-to books on résumé writing begin popping up everywhere. In 1985, background checks become common. In 1987, the fax machine comes into play, and faxing becomes the professional way to send your résumé.

> **1990s:** With the growing use of the World Wide Web, everyone is on email, which means that all résumés are emailed directly to the recipients.

> **2000s:** LinkedIn is founded, and we start posting our résumés online.

What has changed? Well, what we can see from the résumé timeline is that résumés themselves have not changed much, but the way we deliver them has. In the 2010s, we have websites and access to digital media, which enable employers to search for you on Google, Facebook, Twitter, and other platforms. Of course, we also have review-based websites, like Ripoff Report, Mugshots.com, and Yelp, where employers can find information about you (and you can find out about them).

You can think of personal branding as the art of writing your abstract—the summary of your life. What you don't want it to contain is the content you can find about yourself online that appears without your consent. You know: the content you are not proud of, the picture you regret having taken, or even the car accident you were involved in. People will use this content to define you whether the material is relevant or not. We all have a brand already; people have an opinion of us, much of it shaped by what they find and read online—or don't. We need to take back our stories, edit them, rewrite them, and improve them. We can be the narrators of our own digital stories, just as we have historically been the writers of our own résumés.

KNOW WHERE YOU ARE STARTING

Everyone already has a brand online. The difference is that some people control their brand and some people don't. The first step in owning your online presence is to understand what to avoid putting your name on and what not to do online. Then you can start doing the research and working to change what *is* there. If you go through all of the work to tell a beautiful brand story without knowing how to manage it, then you are setting yourself up for failure. When in doubt, stop and ask yourself, If I post this, click this, or connect with this person or thing, who can see it, and what message will it send? If you can't answer, then you should reconsider doing it. Here is a list of actions that I always avoid doing online.

Before you leave a review *anywhere,* think about the consequences it might have, or make sure the account that you are reviewing on is set to Private. I have had clients come in for audits, and when we take a deep dive into their digital footprint, we find unflattering Amazon reviews (some left by their children when the clients left their Amazon accounts open), their scathing reviews of restaurants, or even reviews of their medication on the pharmacy's website. Do yourself a favor: make sure that whatever you are reviewing online while logged in and using your own name isn't something you don't want people to know about.

Don't leave reviews that you don't absolutely mean. I know we all get upset in the moment, but we don't need to blast every person or every company's bad day. Not every review is worth leaving. I have declined to take on clients after finding reviews they wrote online that were unbelievably unnecessary. One potential client had left negative reviews of four different psychiatrists, and one of the doctors actually responded that this person was unwell. The reviews included bold claims—a clear warning to me that gaining this business wasn't worth exposing myself to this person's behavior.

We all have social media and digital accounts that we have lost access to and wish we were able to access for the sole purpose of removing them. Refrain from visiting those websites. For me it's LiveJournal, the online diary for dramatic teenagers in the early 2000s. For some people it's old blogs or Twitter accounts. Don't visit those pages. The more attention you give them, the more relevant they become to the search algorithms.

Just as you would remove your high school and college jobs from your résumé, when you start or redirect your career you should also remove (or make private) the parts of your life that are no longer relevant to your current objective. That picture of you dressed as an alien and drinking cheap wine from a bottle at a college Halloween party is doing nothing for your future. Set the image to Private or For Friends Only.

HOW TO PROPERLY RESEARCH YOURSELF (AND OTHERS)

How the digital world sees you is the way many people who find you online will perceive you as well. This is how the content delivered to you is decided, how the suggested searches you appear in are surfaced, and how your actions online shape who you are perceived to be by certain categories. What you want to do (just as you would do with a résumé) is remove the irrelevant and focus on the best references and parts about yourself.

Do a thorough search and try to find everything you can about yourself online. If you can find it, someone else can get to it, too. When you search for yourself, make sure you are not logged in to Gmail, YouTube, Google, or any other platform, and use an incognito window if you can. This will ensure that you get an unbiased set of results. For a list of websites where you can find out more about what information is online about you, go to pipl.com.

Type in your phone number, email, name, or usernames from social media. The information online may be outdated, so try running a few variations of your searches. For a deeper search and more results, use focused-aggregation search engines, like those listed below, which pool results from several search engines instead of just one at a time. The results may not differ much from what you find on other search engines such as Google, but it is worth doing if you want to find as much as possible. For in-depth social media searches, you can use the Intel Techniques search tool. (We will go over this later.)

» www.dogpile.com

» www.webcrawler.com

» monstercrawler.com

» inteltechniques.com

Let's review all of the information about you that is out there. The goal is to find out as much as possible about your online brand so that you can add, correct, or remove information. Create a content table to keep all of your information in one place. Make your own chart or follow this link to use mine: cynthialive.com/platform. The table should have a column for each of these categories:

What You Don't Want

How Facebook Categorized You

How Google Categorized You

Top Ten Results about You in Search that You Didn't Expect

Once you have filled in the table, look at how many sections match what you have written in the What You Don't Want section. Draw a line through anything that qualifies as something you don't want associated with you and leave everything else to be explored and used as your primary focus, until you add or remove more information. This will help you find the right direction by guiding you away from the wrong one.

Take note of the categories you find yourself in; then start protecting your image and shaping your brand by planning to change them. Here's how.

Amazon

1. Go to www.amazon.com/adprefs.

2. Make sure your advertising preferences are set to Do Not Personalize Ads from Amazon for This Internet Browser.

3. Click Submit.

4. You should get a green box with a check mark that says "Thank you." Your preferences have been saved.

Facebook

1. Go to www.facebook.com/ads/preferences.

2. Click on Your Information to see what information they are using. Then click Your Categories to see how Facebook has categorized your interests.

3. Write these categories down for future reference; then remove the ones you do not want to be associated with by clicking the *X* in the right corner of each.

4. Go back to About You and make sure to remove any information that you don't want them to use.

5. Go to Ad Settings and update each setting to your preference.

6. Go to the Hide Ad Topics section and to the sensitive ads you are targeted for. You can turn these off permanently.

7. You can also suggest other topics to remove permanently in this section.

Here is how Facebook categorized me for reference:

Away from family	New job
Newly engaged (1 year)	Away from hometown
Birthday in January	US politics (very liberal)
Management	Community and Social Services
Facebook access (mobile): all mobile devices	Facebook access (mobile): smartphones
Facebook access (mobile): Apple (iOS)devices	Facebook access (network type): 3G
Gmail users	Facebook access: older devices and OS
Close friends of expats	Facebook access (network type): WiFi
Facebook access (mobile): smartphones and tablets	Technology early adopters
Facebook access (OS): Mac OS X	Engaged Shoppers
Facebook Page admins	Frequent international travelers
Owns: iPhone 7	Frequent Travelers

Google

1. Log in to your Gmail or YouTube account.

2. Go to adssettings.google.com/u/0/authenticated.

3. You should see a list of categories that Google has collected for you.

4. Write them down and then remove the ones that you do not want to be associated with.

5. If you want to turn off your ads personalization (which I suggest), click the slide button in the top right corner of the Ad Personalization box to the left.

6. A box should pop up asking you whether you want to turn these off. Click Turn Off in the bottom right corner. Another box will pop up; click Got It to continue.

Here are my Google categories as an example:

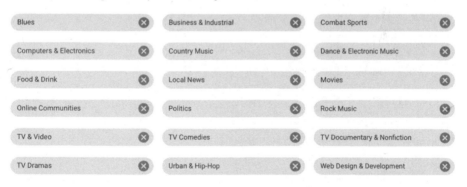

TOPICS YOU LIKE   TOPICS YOU DON'T LIKE (0)

Remove topics you don't like and add ones you do to make the ads you see more useful to you. Topics will also be added as you use some Google services (ex: when you watch a video on YouTube). We're working to include topics from other Google services.

Blues	⊗	Business & Industrial	⊗	Combat Sports	⊗
Computers & Electronics	⊗	Country Music	⊗	Dance & Electronic Music	⊗
Food & Drink	⊗	Local News	⊗	Movies	⊗
Online Communities	⊗	Politics	⊗	Rock Music	⊗
TV & Video	⊗	TV Comedies	⊗	TV Documentary & Nonfiction	⊗
TV Dramas	⊗	Urban & Hip-Hop	⊗	Web Design & Development	⊗

+ NEW TOPIC

For the complete list of advertising settings, go to cynthialive.com/platform

Once you feel like you've done everything to clean up and fix your abstract, ask your mom or the mother-type in your life to do a search on you and find whatever they can. If you get nervous at the thought, you haven't done enough. Go back and keep cleaning.

Consider the narrative that your findings tell about you. Determine what information you want to emphasize and what you want to expunge. Identify the content you wish you could remove, but cannot. Develop a plan for de-emphasizing or suppressing the unremovable content by working with Google to hide specific search results if they are damaging to your character or by proactively creating new content that will appear before the old material in searches. Ways to achieve that are:

- » Joining a new social media platform and becoming active
- » Starting a blog
- » Buying a web domain
- » Interacting on websites you want to be associated with

Assume that everyone will search you before or after you meet. If there is something scathing about you on the internet, don't pretend it isn't there. People will find it, and you should get ahead of it instead of letting them find it first. If you're confronted with regrettable findings in an interview or a meeting, own up to it. Why? Everyone has faults, and honestly, how bad could it be? People will forgive your mistakes, but they won't trust a liar. Make sure you do your research about people you meet with as well. Find out their personal interests, possible connections between you and them, where they went to school, and so forth. Mention something about them to show that you did your research and watch the conversation change.

4 THE FOUR ELEMENTS OF YOUR PERSONAL BRAND

There are four main elements that go into building your personal brand—personal proof, social proof, association, and recognition. Each piece is part of a puzzle, and they all work together to tell a story: your story.

PERSONAL PROOF

The proof that gives you the confidence to go after the next goal, comment on a recent event, and pursue your passions is personal proof.

Examples include:

» Education

» Experience

» Credentials

» Achievements

Personal proof can be difficult to manage, because we all have different metrics for confidence and start at varying confidence levels. Some of us will unknowingly want to put different obstacles in our own way, such as, "I would do A, but I have not completed B, and they may not want me to do A until B has been completed." That reasoning does not make sense. You first have to ask whether you can do A; then and only then should you consider B, once you confirm that B is required for A.

Others will have a different problem: they will want to lie to themselves or others. These people will say, "I have already completed B, so I can do A," even if they have not completed B. People who see no need to prove anything to themselves personally have an easier time taking on commitments that they may not be qualified for.

The people who have a lot of confidence and see less value in the personal proof are those who end up taking the qualified person's job. Of course, there are people who fall somewhere in the middle, but ultimately we all lean in one direction or the other. I have become qualified by jumping into situations for which I was not qualified, because I don't have as much need for personal proof as some do. Those experiences really opened my eyes to how expertise—perceived and actual—factors into modern society. The first time this became evident to me was when I was asked to speak at an executive training event for Fortune 1000 chief marketing officers.

I was excited to be flown to Miami and put up in a nice hotel—all because someone had found me on Twitter. I had to show up a day late to the event because I had previously committed to work I was doing for a charity, which involved many high-profile entertainment professionals. I knew I would be speaking at a roundtable alongside a sponsor and that there would be twelve people in the session. Meeting with the sponsor to go over the details of the first session was one of the most humbling experiences I have ever had. As we talked, I said, "Well, we just want to make sure that we don't go over anyone's head." The sponsor looked at me with a smile, as if he suddenly became aware that I might be out of my element, and said with a laugh, "Oh, we won't be going over their heads."

The next day, I met my cohost in a small room where we waited for the participants to arrive. It was then that I was given the pamphlet that included the other attendees. When I opened it, I almost spewed my coffee across the room. I was hosting a roundtable session with chief marketing officers of some of the most well-known Fortune 500 companies in the world. It hit me then: I was going to be the least qualified, maybe the least educated, and possibly the least prepared person in the room. I wasn't too far off in thinking that. As the room filled up, the session started, and the roundtable flowed with conversation. I found myself in the middle of some of the most interesting conversations I have ever had.

After the session, I had a realization. The discussions I had just been part of was the conversation that people needed to hear, not the nonsense content being pumped out everywhere by people like me, when I was younger and testing ideas to get more clients. They needed stories from people who were the real deal. That day, I started to value my personal proof more than I had done before, and I started my journey to truly understanding personal branding. I wanted to learn how to make these hyperintelligent, driven, and successful people better known. I knew there had to be a better way to make smart, relatable people more visible to the greater population, and to do that I needed to hold myself to a higher standard.

What is included in personal proof? To understand it a bit more in depth, answer the following questions for examples of how these metrics for confidence vary:

The purpose of college or trades' training is?

Did you go to college?

Did you complete a degree?

Do you have a job?

If you have a degree and a job, is your current job in the same field as the degree you earned?

When you interviewed for your job, did they ask for proof that you completed a college degree?

Did they call your references?

What is more important to the person interviewing you—your degree or your references?

I have asked these questions to audiences of many different sizes, ages, and skill levels. Unless doctors, architects, or lawyers are in the room, 99 percent of the participants will say that they have never been asked to prove that they have a degree, that their current job is not what they went to school for, and that their current employer never checked their references. If so few companies check to see whether we went to college and received a degree, why do we wait to get a degree before we look for work? If most of us end up working in an environment unrelated to our degree, then why do we spend money to go to college before we have the opportunity to explore new fields? The answer is personal proof. We need that degree to feel prepared enough to interview. What else does this tell us? It tells us that people care more about whom you know, how you know them, and what they think of you than about what *you* know.

I am not saying that you should not go to college. I am asking that you recognize why you are going or why you went. If you need college to serve as your personal proof that you are educated and capable of greatness, then that's why you do it. I did. I needed it. But if you also know that most people care more about whom you know than what you studied, attending a college that yields the best network and networking opportunities takes on greater meaning and importance.

Personal proof is different for everyone. Here is how I saved two years and $140,000. After I received my bachelor's degree in 2013, at the ripe old age of twenty-six, I felt unstoppable. I went from feeling insecure to acting overly confident. I had already been working at an agency for just over a year, and I made partner a few months after I graduated. A year after I graduated, our agency was acquired by another company, and I began looking into attending business school at a few well-respected institutions. This idea came to me after meeting the chief officers at the Miami event.

I took a bunch of GMAT courses and spent a lot of cash to take them; then I took the GMAT three times and started on my application for a part-time program at one of the schools I was considering. This program involved attendance on weekends and evenings. To my surprise, I received an email from the director of admissions at one of my top-choice executive programs, inviting me to come in for a meeting.

When I sat down for the meeting, the director stared at me for a minute and asked, "How old are you?" I told her that I was nearly twenty-nine. "Looking at your résumé, I expected you to be much older," she replied. I took this as a great compliment, considering that I had just earned my undergrad degree a couple of years ago (with a modest GPA, no less).

She spoke about the program, the level of executive students that come in, and the big companies they come from. Then she asked me the question that made me rethink it all: "Why do you want to get an MBA? Most people who apply to get an MBA are doing it because they want to end up where you are now." I was floored. For the past few years, I had been managing social media accounts, and now I was being asked by one of the top business schools in the country why I would want to attend their program. I said I wanted to learn more about finance, to network, and to have a reason not to travel back and forth to Nashville. (I was working for a company headquartered there.)

After that meeting, I changed my application from the part-time program to the executive program. That is when things got interesting. I started attending executive classes to get a feel for the program. That is when I discovered the greatest hack of all: crashing

MBA classes. I started attending as many of them as I could get to. I would look up the guest speakers and let the school know that I wanted to visit the class as a potential student. During that time, I was becoming increasingly aware that I didn't want to attend business school because the timing was off. I was introduced to a teacher at one of these schools, who had taught there for years and was a trusted source of advice. "You should ride the wave that you are on: save your time, save your money, find a strong chief operating officer, and do your own thing," he said. "The option for an MBA will always be here. The opportunities at your feet now may not be." His advice opened my eyes to an exciting future.

I never applied for business school. Instead, I found teachers and offered to speak to their classes. I have now been a guest lecturer at the University of Southern California, UC Berkeley, Harvard Extension, Vanderbilt, and UCLA's Anderson School of Management. I open every presentation with the following statement: "I don't think I could even get into your school, and today you are paying them to hear me speak. And one day I will have to hire you, because you will know more about many things than I do. Where we are today is not where we will be tomorrow."

For me, personal proof came from asking and hearing the perspectives of the people most involved in the profession that I was considering at the time—people I admired and people who were living a lifestyle that I idolized. I didn't know it at the time, but their opinions were worth more to me than an MBA.

SOCIAL PROOF: WHICH CAME FIRST— THE CHICKEN OR THE EGG?

Social proof is the proof that other people need in order to believe that we are qualified to do something. These are the things that lead people to believe that you can help them, you have something they may want, or they can learn from you. Networking is a selfish game, but not for the reasons that we hear about. For example, CEOs do not want to network with interns; they want to network with other C-suite executives. Producers do not want to network with new actors; they want to network with celebrities. Venture capitalists do not want to network with start-ups; they want to network with investors. This does not mean that all of these people do not need interns or new actors or start-up founders in their circles to do their jobs. It means that people want to network with people on or above their perceived status. However, if you break with traditional avenues and metrics for success, or you have mild success in another circle, then you can network with whomever you like.

EXAMPLES OF SOCIAL PROOF

- » Social media followers
- » Referrals and references
- » Writings as a guest blogger, writing for a major publication, published content, case studies, and so on
- » Speaking engagements and SlideShares
- » Experience doing what you want to do
- » Years of experience, quality of experience, and positive references

ASK UNTIL YOU HEAR "YES"

About two years ago, I asked someone whom I knew how he had started to write for so many different publications. His answer was, "I started a blog and made it really popular with lots of amazing content. Then I started writing for smaller publications and applying to bigger ones. It takes time and a lot of energy. Not very easy to do at all."

I have two problems with his answer. The first is that it infuriates me when someone tells me that what he or she has accomplished is most likely too difficult for me—or anyone else. Again, we are changing the way we think. Support, share the knowledge, and do not glorify yourself.

The second problem I have with his answer is the message that "if it works at all, it will take forever." That is my least favorite answer, ever. I don't like minor things that take a long time. So instead of taking that person's advice and starting a blog full of content that not enough people would read, I went to where I knew I could easily contact people: Twitter.

I searched Twitter for anyone in the United States with the word *editor* in his or her bio. I sent nearly one hundred messages asking the editors if they were looking for contributors. It took me about three hours to send the messages, and I got one response. It sounds pathetic, but the truth is that I only needed one response. An editor at a major publication responded, "We sure are." And just like that, I had gained contributor access in three hours, not three years.

I had no idea what I was going to write about. Presciently, my first article was titled "Your Personal Brand Needs a Growth Strategy." I knew that via writing I could influence topics, help my friends, express myself, add the media outlet's logo to my website under the phrase As Mentioned In, and barter. If I could barter, I could get my clients published in more publications. It was a huge value-add. All of the other endless opportunities that come with writing for a publisher didn't become clear to me until I had that access. Once I had it, I started learning about what it could do.

Was I qualified to write for a major publication at that time? This is debatable, but it wasn't for me to decide: it was up to the editors. For those of you who have no experience, don't use that as a reason not to try. For those of you who have solid experience, be proactive and reach for more opportunity. A ruler's influence can extend beyond the boundaries of the kingdom, but only when the ruler communicates outside those borders.

How to find and connect with editors on Twitter:

1. Log on to www.twitter.com.

2. Decide which publishers you want to get in touch with.

3. In the search bar at the top right of the page, enter the handle for the publication.

4. Get results.

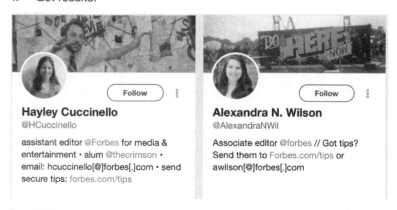

Hayley Cuccinello
@HCuccinello

assistant editor @Forbes for media & entertainment • alum @thecrimson • email: hcuccinello[@]forbes[.]com • send secure tips: forbes.com/tips

Alexandra N. Wilson
@AlexandraNWil

Associate editor @forbes // Got tips? Send them to Forbes.com/tips or awilson[@]forbes[.]com

5. Write down the editors' emails.

6. Follow the editors.

7. Research their work.

8. Retweet their content.

9. Look at their LinkedIn pages.

10. Email them.

HOW TO WRITE FOR PUBLICATIONS

Decide who you want to write for (and why).

Read their contributor guidelines.

Have original, unpublished content ready that fits the guidelines (ideal, but not necessary).

Apply the way the publication requests.

If you don't hear back in a few days, start messaging the publications' editors.

Keep an Excel sheet tracking your submissions and the responses.

SUCCESSFUL BY ASSOCIATION

Association is the part of the personal branding puzzle that determines nearly all of your successes. Why? People decide whether you are credible based on your expertise and your network. You'll need both, and this includes the following:

- » Companies and people you have worked with
- » Blogs and publications you write for
- » Your friends on Facebook
- » Your connections on LinkedIn
- » Anyone you have followed or @messaged on Twitter
- » Anyone who has ever written about you or that you have written about
- » Your family, friends, and acquaintances (good and bad)
- » The schools you've attended and the alumni

» The companies you've worked for and the company you currently work for

» Any organization you volunteer with or support publicly or financially

» Clubs and professional organizations

» Nonprofits and boards that you are on

Association sounds simple, right? You are whom you hang out with. The problem with association in the digital age is that it impacts us more than most people realize. Who is willing to connect with you and how people feel about those people are extremely important. Whom you know, whom you are related to in search, whom you associate with on social media, and so on, are the keys to building your brand. It is extremely important not only to connect with people strategically but also to phrase things in a manner that lets other people know you are associated.

The interesting part about connecting is that one good connection can change your entire network. Instead of reaching the top influencer you hope to connect with, find the person who influences that influencer. Then you have an entirely new group of people at your fingertips *and* you reach your target influencer at the same time.

Volunteer Your Way to Association

Whenever I was told that I couldn't do something or I wasn't right for a certain position or role, I would find a nonprofit organization with a value system I believed in that needed help in the same area I was trying to improve and develop in. The best way to prove you can do something is to do it, but it can be difficult to find a paid opportunity to do so. Volunteering is the way to break in. No one wants to hear about how good you think are or what you think you're capable of. They need to come to that conclusion themselves, and for that to happen, they have to see what you have done.

So do you volunteer just anywhere? No. Volunteer at places that can help you as much as you help them. Do your best, and make sure to talk about the work you've done—for your sake and that of the organization. Don't feel guilty for gaining something in return for your free work. Just don't sign up and underdeliver, or that will become part of your brand story.

SOME SOURCES FOR VOLUNTEER OPPORTUNITIES

» www.volunteermatch.org

» linkedinforgood.linkedin.com/programs/linkedin-members

» www.idealist.org

» Google (search "jobs for volunteers near me")

RECOGNITION—EVERYONE LIKES A PAT ON THE BACK

Being recognized as the best at something and for doing a great job is very important to your abstract and personal brand. It is this recognition that elevates you in the hearts and minds of people everywhere. For example, recognition can include:

» Top lists in media publications such as *Forbes*: "The World's Most Powerful People," "Top People to Follow," and "Tips from 11 Experts"

» Employee of the month

» Top percentile of students in your class

» Traditional awards such as the Nobel Peace Prize, Grammy, Oscar, Gold Medal

» Academic awards

» Local awards

» Military awards

» International recognition

» Anything that shows you were the best at something

Something to remember about recognition is that as you grow or change direction, some forms of recognition become less valuable. For instance, I won the Best Actress award during my junior year in high school. As proud as I am of that, it doesn't help me in what I am doing now or open any new doors. It is important to focus on your goals at each new level and to stop leaning on past accomplishments that are no longer relevant to your new direction.

The Business of Recognition

The crazy thing about awards is that some are given for merit and some are presented for political reasons. In fact, some are completely fictional. That's right. How often do you check to see if a person or company was actually featured by the publisher whose logo they display on their website? Call this out—along with fake awards systems—whenever you see it.

A few years ago, a mentor and colleague nominated me for the *Los Angeles Business Journal* Women's Summit: Rising Star Award. I was honored, not because of the award itself but because someone I admired and looked up to thought enough about me to take the time to nominate me. I got an email from the journal's awards program, informing me that I had been nominated. I was so excited that I did what anyone else would do: I started looking up the judges, the various qualifications for winning, and the past winners. I could not find any information on the qualifications or the judges but only on the prior winners, none of whom had much in common. After a few searches, I assumed that's just the way it's done.

A couple of days passed after I received the nomination email. Then I received a second email, informing me that there were tables to be purchased by my company and that they would be happy to reserve an entire table for a little more than $1,000. The individual tickets were $165 per person. As a nominee I got a free ticket, but everyone else had to pay. I was slightly confused by this, but I was working for a corporate company that had the budget, and we bought a few tickets for others I worked with to attend.

On the day of the event, I was shocked by how many attendees there were, but I was even more shocked by the pamphlet. All of the nominees' names were listed on it, and all of us were given a rose and a glass of champagne. We were then lined up to take individual pictures with an award book that had all the nominees' names on it. After the pictures were taken, we were given a slip of paper that informed us where we could view and purchase the images (taken in terrible lighting, mind you). Irritated from the start because I had given up half my workday, beginning at 7 a.m., to be shuffled around, I walked into the ballroom where the one-hundred-plus tables were located and found our table. We ate some food, listened to some speeches, and waited for the big moment to arrive, when the host began to announce the nominees and the winners. My category was the first one up.

Excited and surrounded by my colleagues, I was disappointed when the host named the winner and only five of the seventy nominees. In that moment, all the nominees probably realized simultaneously that the event was likely a profit generator for the publication and that the selections were possibly political as well. We were all there so that the organizations could benefit from the nominees' social media postings. I was embarrassed, and everyone at my table was embarrassed for me. After we left the event, I did my best not to think about it anymore.

A few weeks went by before the new issue of the *Los Angeles Business Journal* came to the office. My manager (the mentor and colleague who had nominated me) called me into his office and asked if I'd seen the issue. Below the list of winners for each category was a large ad that read "Special Recognition of Cynthia Johnson, Rising Star Nominee." My employer had taken out an ad on the same page that listed the winners, to recognize me in a more prominent way. At that moment I realized what true recognition is: it is having the people who care about you most, whose opinion you care about most, recognize and appreciate you.

Whenever these types of things happen to you, don't discount them. It is fine to say that you were nominated even if a hundred other people were nominated, too. It doesn't take away from you, and many people will still see it as an accomplishment. Post it, share it, and leverage it for as long as it remains relevant. After all, the organization expects to benefit from your affiliation or they wouldn't have created the construct, so you should claim your benefit as well.

5 CREATE YOUR BRAND MESSAGE AND BUILD YOUR DIGITAL ASSETS

Your personal brand message will guide everything you do. It is the statement you will reference whenever you are unsure whether you should do something. The brand statement is your mantra and encapsulates your holistic view. It doesn't just reflect who you are now, it can encompass who you strive to be as well. The best examples of personal brand statements that encompass both personal value and approach to the future can be found in presidential slogans. I know this sounds kind of crazy, but hear me out. Presidential slogans—when they work—are great examples of how individuals can message the focus, passion, and plan that distinguishes them from everyone else.

Some past presidential slogans don't seem as compelling today, but we can attribute this to differences in communication style from one generation to the next. All of them send a clear message that serves as the candidate's personal brand statement.

The slogans from 1884 weren't the greatest, yet it remained the closest election in American history until the 2000 election. Ultimately, Grover Cleveland won.

Cleveland: Blaine, Blaine, James G. Blaine, the Continental Liar from the State of Maine.

Blaine: Ma, Ma, Where's My Pa? Gone to the White House. Ha, Ha, Ha.

These are laughable, song-like campaign slogans, but the candidates' messages—their brand statements—were very clear: Grover Cleveland wanted to prevent Blaine from making it to the White House, and James Blaine wanted to become president.

It turns out that Hillary Clinton wasn't lying about wanting to "build bridges, not walls" in the 2016 presidential race. Evidently her husband, former president Bill Clinton, also wanted to build bridges. In his 1996 campaign against Bob Dole, he told the world that he would "build a bridge to the twenty-first century."

Check out these presidential campaign slogans from 1996.

Dole: The Man for a Better America

Clinton: Building a Bridge to the Twenty-First Century

It's obvious which slogan is better, right? The one with a plan. A presidential campaign slogan needs to identify a plan and a common goal. Bob Dole said that he was "a better man for a better America," which implied that he was some kind of hero. No one likes a guy with a hero complex. If Dole's slogan were also his personal brand statement, he would be an egomaniac. Clinton, on the other hand, seemed to be offering a more abstract message; he was looking to the future with a goal. If Clinton's slogan were also his personal brand statement, he could easily use it as a navigation tool for telling his story and allocating his time.

We are going in reverse here, but Bill Clinton really hit the jackpot in the 1992 election with his running mates and their terrible slogans:

Clinton: Don't Stop Thinking about Tomorrow

Perot: Ross for Boss

By co-opting a Fleetwood Mac lyric, Clinton messaged personality and hopefulness. Perot's message? He wanted to be the boss. No one likes the guy who takes a job just to be the boss. Imagine if they used these personal brand statements to guide their decision making and storytelling. Whom would you want to be friends with, to hire, or to get stuck with in a bar at LAX for six hours?

Now consider the first post–9/11 election with George W. Bush and John Kerry. These were their mantras.

Kerry: Let America Be American Again.

Bush: Yes, America Can!

There's a clear winner here, too. As a brand statement, "Let America Be America Again" just sounds like a crazy guy talking to himself. Who was not letting America be America? If it were Kerry's personal brand statement, he would be lost. "Yes, America Can!" was more a reminder and a reassurance—still not the best, but better than Kerry's.

Now fast-forward to 2016 and the election that really brought personal branding into the mainstream.

Trump: Make America Great Again

Clinton: I'm with Her

Trump is a master when it comes to personal branding, and it showed. I don't know what his personal brand statement is, but if it's "Make America Great Again," he should be fairly clear in his objectives. Hillary Clinton, on the other hand, did not have a clear brand message. It read as self-focused and ambiguous. If "I'm with Her" were her personal brand statement, it would be a difficult message to parse. (You are with her because you *are* her, so is your mission automatically accomplished?)

When creating your personal brand statement, you want to keep it short, simple, clear, and actionable. You want it to have enough meaning that you could not only use it as your slogan in a presidential campaign but also believe in it enough to win an election.

Your personal brand slogan does not have to be unique; you just have to believe in it. In 1980, Ronald Reagan's campaign slogan was "Let's Make America Great Again," and Donald Trump's 2016 campaign slogan was simply "Make America Great Again." In 2008, Barack Obama's winning campaign slogan, "Yes, We Can," was similar to George W. Bush's 2004 campaign slogan, "Yes, America Can!" So to create a winning brand statement, remember that it doesn't matter which side you're on. What counts is how you interpret your brand statement. If you make it actionable and clear, you can use it as the driving force behind the narrative of your personal brand.

My personal brand statement: "Build a Platform for Change"

Now, let's write your personal brand statement.

Consider the following:

> What is your niche? What do you want to be known for as a thought leader?

> Who are the people in your niche who already have a profile or personal brand?

> How can you be clear while being unique?

> Who needs to know about you? Why should they care?

> How do your influencers currently perceive you? (If you don't know, ask.)

> What is your brand voice? Are you funny, direct, relatable, or . . . ?

YOU HAVE TO TELL YOUR STORY BEFORE YOU CAN ADVISE SOMEONE ELSE

Part of personal branding is helping to craft your own story so that no one else does it for you. You want to be the strongest and most vocal advocate for yourself. In this era, most people never have the opportunity to defend themselves because few of us will ask the person directly, for fear of drawing more attention. Instead, we search for the person online and use whatever we find to make our own judgment calls about the individual.

This works in the opposite direction as well. If you want to join a club, get into college, get a job, join a board, work with a nonprofit, get an investor for your company, or even get invited to a private party, who you are online can affect the outcome. If you tell someone you are one thing, but they see something else online, it can have a terrible affect on your life without your even knowing it. Consider this example. You are the best lawyer for a high-profile case. You went to Harvard and have a great success record in the courtroom. But when I pull up your LinkedIn account, you have only fifty connections, and your Facebook feed has a tagged photo of you drinking at karaoke. I would question your résumé.

You have to create the best possible story about yourself in order to convey that to the people researching you online. If you wouldn't put it on a résumé or hang it in a frame in your living room, you shouldn't post it online.

This strategy is not to make you seem inauthentic. Résumés and the pictures you hang in your living room represent two major parts of who you are: your career and your most precious moments. Each of these represents how you spend your time—the strongest indicator of who you are as an individual. If you are not on social media all of the time, no problem. Set up your accounts, double-check your security settings, and let them sit. If you love social media, just be mindful of what is visible to the public. The person you were five years ago (let alone ten years ago) is probably not the same person you are today, so update your older content as you would with your résumé and framed pictures.

ONLINE RESOURCES FOR CRAFTING YOUR MESSAGE

These can change over time. Check websites for updates.

Websites and Apps to Improve Your Digital Storytelling

shorthand.com: tell beautiful digital stories

flourish.studio: visualize and tell stories with data

hemingwayapp.com: write with more boldness and clarity

grammarly.com: improve your grammar and spelling

Writing Tools

copyscape.com: check for plagiarism

headlines.sharethrough.com: write better headlines

cliche.theinfo.org: search your stories for clichés

Finding Expert Resources

scholar.google.com

sources.npr.org

expertisefinder.com

theglobalexperts.org

womensmediacenter.com

Facts and Research

embassyworld.com: find embassies around the world

projects.propublica.org/nonprofits: search nonprofits' financial information

highbeam.com: find articles, magazines, research papers

city-data.com: find city statistics

continued

Politics

openstates.org: find policies and policy makers

opensecrets.org: see where political donations came from

darkmoneywatch.org: find dark political donations

popvox.com: find, support, or oppose bills proposed to Congress

Just for Fun

ctrlq.org/first: find out who tweeted something first

content.time.com/time/magazine/coversearch: search for previous covers of *TIME* magazine

radio.com: create your own internet radio show

interviews.televisionacademy.com/interviews: find old television interviews

Building Online Assets

Building your social media profiles and online communities is tedious. It can be time consuming, frustrating, and difficult when you don't know how to do it any other way than manually. The tendency is to push these tasks aside and try not to think about them. That is the wrong approach. Avoiding the foundational part of your personal brand will only lead to more work later on.

The first thing to consider when you start building your online profile is your name. Actually, the very first thing you should do is hire someone else to do the initial audit and cleanup (try Upwork or Taskrabbit) because it is really tedious and boring. Whether you hire someone or do it yourself (again, I don't suggest this because too often people get overwhelmed and give up), you should have an understanding of what to look for and what to do.

The first step is picking a name or variation of your name that you can use on all or most of your social media pages. You don't want to have to go into every single social media site to see if your name is available: that is way too much work. Instead, you can browse websites such as Namechk or KnowEm to see if your name is available and where to claim all of your profiles at once. You won't be active on all of these profiles, but you never know when you will want to be active on a site later. This is why claiming your name once and permanently is so important.

Namechk's tool allows you to look up your desired name and then search through hundreds of social media sites that tell you which ones are available and which ones are not, using the name that you searched for.

KnowEm does the same thing as Namechk, but it also looks for domain names (website names that are available using your desired name) and checks the United States Patent and Trademark Office database to see if the trademark is available as well.

If you insist on setting up your own social media websites and not using KnowEm, make sure to include the following sites on your list to claim your name:

About.me

AngelList

Facebook
(personal account)

Google Plus

Instagram

LinkedIn

Medium

Pinterest

Product Hunt

Reddit

SlideShare

Telegram

Twitter

WordPress

YouTube

PURCHASE A DOMAIN NAME

You should have a website for your brand, and that website needs a name. You can use websites such as whois.net, Check-Domains.com, GoDaddy, or Instant Domain Search to find out whether the domain name you want is available or, if it is not available, who owns it so that you can attempt to buy it.

Ideally you want to buy a domain that is your real full name, like cynthiajohnson.com, but if you have a common name like I do, that domain may be either taken or very expensive to purchase. The other thing you want to remember is that .com domains are really the only domains you want to purchase for your personal brand website. Don't pick .org, .net, or anything that seems cute or clever, like .social. Always use .com.

If your name is not available, then choose a variation of your name. Make this as simple as possible. Remember that you want to keep at least part of your name in the domain name, otherwise it defeats the purpose of personal branding.

Once you have decided on your domain name, you want to buy that name in .net, .co, and .org so that other people can't use those domains, and you'll have the option to use them later if you choose. If these domain names are not available, don't worry; this is more of an additional and optional step.

If you do end up buying those other domains, make sure to redirect them to your .com address. Redirecting works by sending users to the .com address when they type in the .net address.

How I Ended Up with Cynthialive.com

My first internship in digital marketing was with a company called Live Citizen. Their website was a social media community for citizen journalism and polling focused on politics. My Twitter name became @cynthialive because at the time I was representing Live Citizen. My job as an intern was to blog about what was happening on the website, manage their social media, and use the @cynthialive username to gain more users on Live Citizen. Twitter is an obvious choice for a political website to work from because it is used a lot in political media coverage.

When the website shut down, I took my @cynthialive name and made it my personal Twitter name, because @cynthiaj and @cynthiajohnson were not available. Then when I went to purchase a domain name for my personal website, I found that no one was using cynthiajohnson.com, but someone owned it. I contacted the owner of the domain, who asked for twenty thousand dollars to sell me the domain (and this was back in 2010). I did not have—nor would I ever spend—twenty thousand dollars for a website name.

I decided to use cynthialive.com to match my Twitter profile. Since it was available and used my name, I went with it. When you get ready to create your domain name, don't fret if you aren't able to get it. Be creative, and you will find something else that can work just as well.

BUILDING A WEBSITE

Once you have your domain purchased, you will need to build a website. You can choose one of several ways to do this. If you are not experienced in website building, you can always turn to companies such as Wix, Weebly, or Squarespace and use one of their premade templates. This option is not ideal because it's not as distinctive as designing something original, but it works.

Another option is a WordPress template, using wordpress.org not wordpress.com. You would go to www.wordpress.org and download WordPress. You would then install WordPress with your website host. For a step-by-step guide on how to build your own website, go to cynthialive.com/platform.

What you can do is contact a web developer (try Upwork to find one) and have them build a custom WordPress theme for you. This is a more expensive route but definitely the best way to go for an optimal website.

WHAT TO INCLUDE ON YOUR WEBSITE

If you are not trying to make money by selling items on your site, there is no reason for you to have a long, blog-driven website. You maybe need to post once every few weeks (if the content seems relevant). Check out a sample schedule for personal brand blogging at cynthialive.com/platform

You will also need an About section for your biography, companies you are associated with, awards, and personal interests—the basis of your online résumé. You will need a section for press mentions or media as well: anything that involves you in the news, including blogs you were interviewed in, websites you have guest written for, podcasts you've done, and so forth. (This coverage does not have to be only from large mainstream outlets.)

The next part is especially important. Depending on whether you want to be paid to speak or your business directly benefits from your speaking and you don't mind doing some for free, you will need to include "Invite me to speak" or "Hire me to speak" on your website. This separation is extremely helpful for sorting through and vetting new opportunities. At first this may not seem like a huge priority, but as you become more known, your time will become more and more difficult to manage. When someone contacts you about media or speaking, there are two ways to handle it when you are not represented by a speaking agent. You can answer all of the emails yourself and negotiate your own terms, or you can create a second email address such as media@yourwebsite.com. Use this address to negotiate your rates as your assistant would do for you. This makes it easier to quote and negotiate your preferred rates.

You want to make sure that you have a Contact Me page. If people cannot contact you, then there is less benefit in having a website. Create a contact email for your website that is yourname@yourwebsite.com; for example, I am cynthia@cynthialive.com. This is much more professional and easier to remember than a Gmail or other email provider–based address.

Types of Opportunities, What to Expect, and How to Prepare for Them

Personal branding opportunities come in many forms. Some are easy to recognize as opportunities and others are not. This is when focusing on and separating the four elements of your brand becomes important. At different stages of your brand evolution, you will need more opportunities in one area than another.

In addition to a website, you should create a media kit, get a headshot, and have a short (150-word) bio as well as a full bio ready. That way when new opportunities present themselves, you can easily send over the required materials. It is also helpful to have three presentations in bullet outline form that can also be readily sent out. Knowing exactly whom you can speak to and whom you want to speak to, along with having a prepackaged press kit to send out, will make a world of difference in your outreach efforts.

As your brand changes and you change, it may become increasingly important that you gain more education and knowledge in a specific area. This would be your personal proof. Types of personal proof include taking classes, networking at niche-topic events, having conversations with people who are doing what you want to be doing, and even relocating to another part of the world. Doing something that is self-directed can provide personal proof. When interning, for example, take on a project as an assistant so you can learn how to do something new, or set and accomplish goals in an area before you start taking on work in that area. These are opportunities to learn and build confidence while testing your interest in the new direction you seek.

Courses that are helpful to people who are building a brand include speech-writing and neuro-linguistic programming (NLP) for speech and negotiation. I learned the most useful tools for brand management in acting improvisation classes, which taught me to be well informed and quick on my feet.

Look for mentors, free workshops, and opportunities to test your abilities in ways that will have minimal negative effects on you. Create your own panel sessions to see if you are able to be on a successful panel. Practice speaking in front of people and the camera by offering your time to clubs and organizations that hold events for their members.

PLACES TO FIND OPPORTUNITIES FOR PERSONAL PROOF

Education

Coursera
Coursera has a lot of classes on a range of different topics. Their classes are usually inexpensive and sometimes even free. You can also use Coursera to build and sell your own online education platform.

Curious
Curious enables you to learn something new every day. The site offers daily brain workouts for sixty-nine dollars per year.

Lynda (now LinkedIn Learning)

Lynda.com was acquired by LinkedIn before LinkedIn was acquired by Microsoft. The classes are professionally edited and constructed, and the teachers are picked by Lynda. You can access all of their classes for twenty-five dollars per month.

Sitepoint

Sitepoint opens all of their classes for as little as five dollars per month, depending on when you sign up. The classes focus on digital marketing, search engine optimization (SEO), WordPress, Design, and JavaScript.

Skillshare

The prices to go Pro on this website or buy for an entire team are very inexpensive, ranging from free to fifteen dollars per month. You can take classes on everything from design, web development, and business to culinary arts and entertainment.

Udemy

Udemy is growing at a rapid pace. They add hundreds of new classes every month. But their classes can be more expensive, ranging from ten to five hundred dollars per class.

Networking

» Meetup

» Eventbrite

» Facebook

» Eventful

» Google (search for "networking events in my area")

SOCIAL PROOF—WHEN YOU LEAST EXPECT IT

Social proof is what stands between you and what you want. Social proof opportunities come randomly, and you often have to recognize and claim them before you feel fully prepared to do so.

Once, when I could not fly to speak at an educational council in the Philippines, I had to cancel my appearance at the last minute. I was the guest of honor and the only international attendee, so my inability to attend was a big deal for the event organizers. Instead of Skyping into the event or leaving the organizers to figure out a replacement, I called a couple of people who I knew wanted to break into international speaking. One of them accepted; the others said they didn't feel quite ready. When I asked the person who accepted why he was so willing to fill in at the last minute (for an unpaid engagement), he said that if he spoke at the event, he would then be able to say that he was an international speaker. So it was well worth it for him to change his schedule to attend.

That was the most honest and intuitive answer he could have given. The events and opportunities that have yielded the most return for me are those in which I filled in for someone unexpectedly, felt unprepared, or had to move quickly without much thought. Social proof can be hard to gain, because it requires that you do the very thing you do not want to do in order to do the thing you want to do. That's why you have to see beyond the event or the moment when you feel unprepared and out of your element, and then push through to gain that experience.

Association is the easiest type of opportunity to miss. It requires showing up even when you are exhausted. It means offering help and even giving up on a preference that is actually less valuable. The opportunity to be part of something that would help catapult your career and life to the next level is almost always worth taking.

ORGANIZATIONS TO BUILD ASSOCIATION

It can be helpful to join clubs and organizations if you are willing to give the time or money they require. Here are a few organizations you can join. (Not all of these will apply to everyone, but they are good examples of what to look for.)

American Marketing Association (AMA)
You can pay to join several of the American Marketing Association's local chapters to attend events, write industry papers, and add to your résumé.

Entrepreneurs' Organization (EO)
The Entrepreneurs' Organization (EO) is a global network that works to enhance the ability of entrepreneurs to be successful by learning and growing from the knowledge and experience of other members.

Forbes Councils
Want to write for *Forbes*? You may qualify for one of their many councils, such as the finance council, agency council, business development council, and human resources council. You can apply and pay them a fee of twelve hundred to fourteen hundred dollars per year to gain access to everyone in the councils and their Forbes Council Facebook group, and to write for *Forbes* regularly. The councils evolve—and sometimes move locations—over time, but members are kept intact.

Ivy
Ivy is a social organization that charges one thousand dollars per year to attend events, host webinars, and reach their large global network of successful people in several industries.

continued

The Millennium Alliance

The Millennium Alliance is a leading technology, business, and education advisory firm. It focuses in areas such as business transformation, executive education, growth, policy, and need analysis for C-level executives from Fortune 1000 companies. (I sit on their board of advisors.)

Vistage

Vistage is for CEOs and companies that want to improve and grow their businesses through idea exchange. They have more than eighteen thousand members and host more than sixteen thousand events each year.

Young Entrepreneur Council (YEC)

The Young Entrepreneur Council is another membership-based organization that you can join if you want to write for *Forbes*, *Huffington Post*, Business.com, and several other publications, or get media mentions, network with other entrepreneurs, attend events, and more. The fee is eight hundred to twelve hundred dollars per year. To qualify, you have to be founder or partner at an organization with more than $1 million in annual revenue or that sold for more than $1 million.

There are many more organizations and nonprofits like these that you could join to grow your network and increase your opportunities through association. It sounds expensive to join some of them, but depending on your unique and specific goals, it can be well worth it.

Opportunities for Recognition

The biggest mistake people make when it comes to missed opportunities for recognition is thinking that the opportunity is too small. No opportunities are too small to be recognized. Podcast interviews, blog mentions, awards from small local community organizations and events—these are all accomplishments. It doesn't take much time to accept an award or to do an interview. Plus, the smaller opportunities are the best way to practice and prepare for the larger ones. Build the online foundation for your brand by creating opportunities and converting those experiences into reportable qualifications.

WHERE TO FIND OPPORTUNITIES FOR RECOGNITION

Check out the websites below to find opportunities to speak, be interviewed for podcasts, and apply for awards.

awardshub.com
This service matches you and your business with awards and submits your name for consideration.

listennotes.com
With this podcast search engine, you can find dozens of podcasts by topic or prior guests, along with the websites where you can contact the hosts and submit yourself as a potential interviewee.

speakerhub.com
You can use this service to either create a speaker profile and submit yourself as a potential speaker or find a speaker for your next event.

speakermatch.com
This service creates your profile and provides a nice dashboard to manage your submissions to be a speaker. Their fees range from as low as ten dollars per month to about eight hundred dollars per year.

Bring Your Offline Experiences Online to Benefit Your Digital Brand

I know many people who host events, attend events, and travel all over the world for work, yet no one in their network ever hears about it. If you win an award and no one knows about it, did it really happen? Whenever you go to an event or take a class, it doesn't require much effort to snap a picture with someone else there and post it immediately to social media.

Another thing I like to do is check in to events on social media as I am leaving. This attaches me to the event and lets my audience know I was there. When you check in as you are leaving, you avoid telling the world where you are (which is much safer than checking in as you arrive at a location). Plus, when you have checked in to an event as you are leaving, you will presumably have images that you can add to the post, so you can avoid having to post twice.

I like to check in on Facebook, Twitter, and Instagram and to send a snap mid-event or on my way out. When I am flying somewhere, I check in from the airport with the destination included as I am boarding the flight. If I am speaking at a conference or hosting an event, I will check in earlier and tag my friends.

These are simple ways that busy people can utilize their offline work online. If you are not a fan of checking in on social media, then post after the event and tag other attendees, the host, and any sponsors or speakers. After an event, I will post to LinkedIn, Twitter, Facebook, and, occasionally, Instagram (depending on the quality of the images I took).

WHAT COUNTS AS AN EFFECTIVE BRAND IMAGE FOR SOCIAL MEDIA?

Personal brand images are most effective when they present you doing something interesting, show you somewhere interesting, show you being the best at something (such as speaking or being interviewed), show you with someone interesting, or demonstrate your day-to-day while sending a strong positive message.

Images with other people you can tag or at events that you can tag are the best option. Grab a picture with someone at an event. Don't be shy about asking. They are there to please the crowd. And if you are the speaker, let people take pictures with you. They will always want to, and that is part of the fun of seeing someone speak at a conference.

The other way to make sure that your offline work connects online is to connect with people from the events you attend. The main point of events, meet ups, and conferences is to network. Afterward, it is fine to send a request to connect on LinkedIn with the message: "We didn't have a chance to connect at [Event Name]. We should connect here and make time to speak when it works for our schedules."

People like to be noticed, especially the people who attend these types of events. By using the conference or meet up as your way to connect, you are finding common ground, which makes your out-reach that much easier.

6 RUMOR HAS IT

Rumors are the worst, especially when your reputation—your brand—is at the center of one. What happens when a rumor begins to surface? It can result from a terrible game of telephone, a misunderstanding, a person's mood, or an intentional lie started by one person about another. Can rumors ever be helpful?

I figured that any behavior as commonplace as rumormongering must have an explanation in behavioral science. I was half right. In early 1942, the US government under President Franklin Roosevelt began to worry about the spread of rumors about the war and how they would affect public opinion concerning the United States and its soldiers. By this time in the war, Germany and the other countries that made up the Axis powers were using rumors (mostly being spread by common, well-intentioned people) as psychological warfare with the intent to cause panic and chaos.

Examples of rumors being spread according to the New England Historical Society:[8]

> Indian soldiers at Fort Devens were raping women.

> No US Navy vessels survived Pearl Harbor.

A woman's head exploded after she permed her hair and went to work in a shell factory.

Unmarried pregnant women in the Women's Auxiliary Army Corps were sent home from North Africa.

With so much at stake, it made sense that the United States would have tried to find a way to combat these rumors. On June 13, 1942, President Roosevelt signed an executive order to create the Office of Wartime Information (OWI). The goal of the OWI was to slow the spread of false information and promote "positive" information. Part of the OWI's strategy included the creation of a radio broadcast called *Voice of America* (which is operating today) and to introduce something called "Rumor Project."

The Rumor Project plan included "rumor clinics." The rumor clinics were to be set up across the United States at universities and colleges and run by a selected group of students and professors. These volunteers would study media and news, and report the information back to the OWI. The OWI identified eight potential locations for their rumor clinics, including one in Boston to be run by psychologist Robert Knapp.

The OWI and social scientists were unable to successfully work together. The OWI wanted to control the clinics and the social scientists wanted to perform research based on their own guidelines. Robert Knapp, who was acting as a consultant to the OWI along with his former teacher, psychologist Gordon Allport, had already launched their own rumor clinic in partnership with the *Boston Herald*, despite the OWI's effort to end the psychologists' program. The OWI plan to launch their rumor clinics never got off the ground.

Knapp and Allport continued their research at the jointly named *Boston Herald* Rumor Clinic. The clinic surfaced the most notorious rumors of the week and the newspaper printed them on the front page, where journalists discussed and disapproved of them.

After the war, in 1947, Gordon Allport and Leo Postman published their research from the rumor clinics in a book entitled *The Psychology of Rumor*.[9] They defined rumors as "propositions of faith on specific (or current) topics that pass from person to person, usually by word of mouth, without any evidence of their truth."

Here are the findings about rumors from the published research by Allport and Postman.

> Rumors are spread by mouth.

> Rumors provide information about people, events, and conditions (circumstances surrounding something or someone).

> Rumors meet the emotional needs of a person or community.

> Rumors rely on the emphasis given to their characteristics; that is, "How well does the rumor fit in with what I need or want to hear today?" Examples of these characteristics include:
> » Is the word of mouth backed by the media? (Does TMZ also believe that Elvis is alive? Do they talk about the possibility?)
>
> » Is the rumor full of content found publicly versus privately? (Is the rumor about your mother or Donald Trump? I'm not saying that your mother isn't newsworthy, but the Donald Trump rumor has more legs.)
>
> » Are people listening and responding emotionally? (Did Elvis fake his own death? Or is the rumor in response to the emotional need of his fans to understand his death? I'm not saying that it's impossible, but for the sake of this argument, let's say it was a rumor.)

So we know that rumors require word of mouth, that they need extra media attention to spread, and that when you add emotional needs to the mix, these fabrications spread like wildfire.

Robert Knapp took the liberty of collecting various rumors and dividing them into categories based on their content.

Impossible Dream Rumors

These are pipe dreams—rumors that we wish were true but are simply not possible. Consider these, for example, "There won't be a test on Friday because the teacher will be sick," or, "No one will fire me because I am related to the boss."

Ghost Rumors

These are fear-based rumors concerning ghosts, monsters, and the like. Bigfoot, the Jersey Devil, or any alien entity that has ever been discussed on *The X-Files* is sure to fall into this category.

Rumors That Lead to Disagreements

These rumors are used to ruin relationships and undermine alliances. Some examples are the tactics used on the reality show *Survivor* and lies spread to break up a friendship or marriage.

Knapp found that negative rumors spread faster than positive ones. One example of a positive rumor resulted from me telling my mother that my internship was with a social media company. "Social media, you know?" I said. "Like Facebook." She then proceeded to tell the rest of the family that I worked for Facebook. Considering that it was 2010, this made me very popular with my extended family, which I was unaware of until years later, when my cousin asked me about my position at Facebook. (If you ever need a positive rumor to be spread about yourself, tell your mom.)

RUMOR MILLS

There is much more to discuss about rumors and their effects on our lives, both past and present, and how we can combat the negative effects with our personal brands. It turns out that Allport and Postman (authors of *The Psychology of Rumor*) created a mathematical formula for the basic law of rumors. The formula states that the strength of the rumor is linked to its importance and degree of ambiguity:

$$R = i \times a$$

Great. These gentlemen told us everything we need to know about how a rumor works and how to categorize it, but the formula for grading it is a bit difficult to understand. What I want to know is, How do rumors get started?

NPR *Science* ran a podcast episode titled "How Do Rumors Get Started?"[10] The episode included expert guests Nicholas DiFonzo, coauthor of *Rumor Psychology: Social and Organizational Approaches*, and Duncan Watts, author of *Six Degrees: The Science of a Connected Age*.

Who Starts Rumors?

The short answer is anyone and everyone. In fact, according to Watts, "There needn't be anything particularly special about the person who starts the rumor, and so this is sort of a bit counterintuitive, because when something special happens—when some, you know, amazing rumor starts sort of sweeping across a city or a country or even throughout an organization, you might think that the person who began it had to be special as well. But that actually turns out not to be the case necessarily."

What *does* have an impact on starting rumors, according to Watts, is social networking. Social networks connect many groups of people, irrespective of geographical location, and these groups, not the individuals, magnify the spread of rumors.

Why Do Rumors Start?

This is the biggest question of all. Many times the start of a rumor is due to misinformation; however, it spreads because there is no formal information to counter it. DiFonzo told NPR listeners that "the best way to get rumors going in an organization is to not say anything or to not say very much or to say contradictory things."

WHAT DO RUMORS HAVE TO DO WITH PERSONAL BRANDING?

What you don't put online and what you don't say are just as important, if not more important, than what you put online and comment on. We live in a world where most of us search for people online before meeting them, before hiring them, or when we are just plain bored. We also live in a world where our friends and family tag us online, our companies put our faces on their websites, everyone has a camera, social media and search engines use face recognition, and our phones track us everywhere we go. All of these things make anonymity extremely difficult—and in some instances nearly impossible—for many people.

For those of us who wish to lead private lives and be anonymous in today's world, personal branding is about being strategic in what you say about yourself, not saying nothing at all. The more information you put out there about yourself, the less room there is for misinterpretation. Formal information has now become extremely important.

For instance, my strategy was to post only the exciting things that happened to me at work. I would post news about my job, articles about my job, and pictures of myself at work events. The results were shocking. Everyone in my life (including my grandmother) constantly talked to me about work. The people geographically closest to me, whom I spent most of my time with, were the only people who knew anything about me outside of work. People I would see on random occasions or play catch-up with at weddings started telling me how proud they were of my success and asking me how I achieved it. The truth is that when I started this experiment, I was no more successful than the average twenty-six-year-old. I may even have been less successful financially and professionally than most of the people I knew, but that was not what people thought about me.

When I got engaged, I posted it on social media. Many people whom I knew and saw regularly, from work or at random local events, didn't even know that I was in a relationship because I kept my Facebook content focused on work—so much so that Facebook is convinced that I am either a single straight man or a single lesbian woman.

This level of commitment to share only one type of content was incredibly valuable for my career. When all anyone knew about me was that I had a job I cared about and that I spoke about my craft, and when the only images they saw of me showed me speaking at a conference or with another speaker at a conference, they assumed I was an expert in my field. My personal life remained completely private, leaving no room for interpretation about my professional abilities.

WILL THE REAL EXPERTS PLEASE SPEAK UP?

Rumors will spread when there isn't enough formal information to dispel them. Fake news is not new, and neither are fake experts. What *is* new is the increasing number of people who have the ability to create and share news. Have you ever watched or listened to someone on television or radio being interviewed on a topic about which you consider yourself an expert, only to realize halfway into the interview that this person knows less than you do? If so, or if you can imagine this situation, how would you respond? Would you call the television or radio host (given that we all have instant access and the ability to find anyone's contact information) and tell them that their guest should be more expert? Would you ignore it? If you hear someone sharing fake expertise, and you are an expert on the topic, you have missed your opportunity if you do nothing.

Whenever you see or hear a story with incorrect or misleading information from a less-than-credible expert, or a story that could benefit from your expert opinion, reach out to the editor, the media company, the host, or the writer. Inform these people of the misprint or mistake, give them the correction, and let them know why you are a credible source. If you do have expertise in that area, they are indeed incorrect, *and* they are also receptive, they should gladly make the edit. Most journalists do not intentionally misrepresent the truth; however, many talking heads are misrepresented as journalists. Offer your edit and let the media company or journalist know that they can contact you for advice and commentary on future content in your area of expertise. After working with certain news organizations awhile, you may even get paid to be on call for comments on future stories.

In short, if you truly are an expert, then exert your expertise—don't let others command the attention when you could do better.

HOW CAN YOU COMPETE WITH SELF-PROCLAIMED EXPERTS?

If you want to build a credible personal brand that allows you to be in a position of authority to dispel bias or false information, you have to understand how and why people find other people credible. Many people who are recognized experts on a topic have been doing it for so long that they've forgotten how valuable their knowledge is. They find it difficult and even disrespectful to their colleagues to speak about themselves as experts. Don't let yourself fall for that thinking.

To be taken seriously and to work toward building an effective, authoritative personal brand, you need to take yourself seriously, evoke authority, and provide more detail, not less.

In "The Russian 'Firehose of Falsehood' Propaganda Model," research scientists Christopher Paul and Miriam Matthews at the RAND Corporation discuss the peripheral cues that make people appear credible to others.[11] According to them, the field of psychology shows that cues such as the apparent expertise of the source and the format of information can lead people to automatically accept that it is coming from a credible source. The peripheral route also operates when a message contains many arguments (information overload), and listeners are persuaded because they lack the ability or motivation to process all of it. These peripheral cues are shortcuts to increased credibility.

On the internet, peripheral cues are considered a form of Poe's Law, an internet law that holds that unless you add some form of smiley face at the end of any statement, the reader can perceive it as true (credible) no matter how outlandish it may be. So if you're going to tell a joke, make it clear that you are joking. For example, if you say something in a sarcastic tone, when you are quoted later, it will be read by people who can't hear your tone. For more examples of Poe's Law, read this subreddit: reddit.com/r/poeslawinaction/.

People who claim to be experts will have an easier time being believed than experts who don't claim the title. According to Paul and Matthews, "Expertise and trustworthiness are the two primary dimensions of credibility, and these qualities may be evaluated based on visual cues, such as format, appearance, or simple claims of expertise."

The RAND research scientists also found that "online news sites are perceived as more credible than other online formats, regardless of the veracity of the content." This is why bylines in third-party publications will always be greater indicators of authority, and why personal blogs should be used more for communicating with an audience or for building an authoritative website. In personal branding, a third-party byline or endorsement will always lend more credibility, so it should be even more of a priority than your own website.

When individuals have experience and expertise, they tend to over-estimate their audiences' knowledge on the subject and, in an effort not to overwhelm them with information, they avoid providing many details. This is the exact opposite of what they need to do. According to Paul and Matthews, "In courtroom simulations, witnesses who provide more details—even trivial details—are judged to be more credible."

A CASE STUDY: GOSSIP CHANGES THE WAY OUR BRAINS PERCEIVE PEOPLE

In an NPR report entitled "Psst! The Human Brain Is Wired for Gossip," Jon Hamilton discusses a study conducted by Lisa Feldman Barrett, a professor of psychology at Northeastern University.[12] Her research examined how gossip affects what we know and how we feel about an unfamiliar person. The question Barrett's team set out to answer was, "Once gossip has predisposed us to see someone in a certain light, is it possible for us to see them in a different light?"

The researchers gathered a group of volunteers and asked them to look at the faces of random people. The faces were paired with random bits of gossip, some positive and some negative.

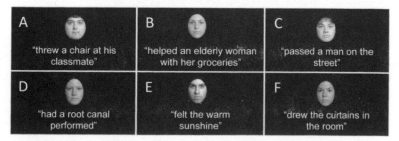

Participants in the study were shown a neutral face paired with (A) negative gossip, (B) positive gossip, (C) neutral gossip, (D) negative nonsocial information, (E) positive nonsocial information, and (F) neutral nonsocial information. When the study participants viewed the faces again, their brains were more likely to fix on the faces associated with negative gossip.

The research team showed each volunteer two sets of pictures at the same time. The left eye would see one image while the right eye would see a different one. For instance, the left eye might be looking at a picture of a face while the right eye was looking at a picture of a car. They did this to test how the volunteers' brains reacted to the different kinds of information. This scientific method—the process of showing two extreme opposite images—causes something called binocular rivalry, since the human brain is capable of processing only one image at a time. So we will unconsciously lean toward one image and focus on it for longer.

The researchers discovered that when they did this, the volunteers would spend more time on the pictures where a face was paired with a negative piece of gossip than on pictures where a face was paired with a positive piece of gossip. This suggests that our brains are wired to focus our attention on someone more if we are told a pejorative detail about them. Barrett's team was able to demonstrate how secondhand information about a person can have an enormous effect. In essence, gossip helps us to predict friends and foes.

Another professor of psychology, Frank McAndrew, from Knox College in Galesburg, Illinois, and other researchers have posited that human interest in gossip results from evolutionary development, not poor character. Professor McAndrew attributes this to primitive times when humans lived together in small groups. Prehistoric humans needed to be able to identify threats within the community, where waiting to decide for themselves would have taken too much time and exposed them to more danger. The fastest way to determine whether someone was a threat to the group was through word-of-mouth communication, or gossip.

We now know that gossip has an actual effect on our brains. It is not just an individual experience of how we think about and digest gossip. Our brains are hardwired to be extra cautious around people we have heard negative stereotypes about. Without a counter-effect for these negative and potentially harmful rumors, we become powerless against a problem we may not even know we have.

CASE STUDY: DOCTORS ON SOCIAL MEDIA

We have explored why we should create and populate our social media profiles with positive information. For example, we know that we want to combat negative rumors, online content that we did not post or authorize, and the occasional legal document from a few years back. In this case study, we are going to explore how the content that we post on social media and blog websites can impact our careers.

In an article on United Press International (UPI), Amy Horton discusses a study that looked at the social media presence of newly graduated urologists. The study was conducted by Dr. Kevin Koo, a urology resident at the Dartmouth-Hitchcock Medical Center in Lebanon, New Hampshire.[13] Koo and his team searched Facebook for the names of 281 doctors who had graduated from urology residency programs in the United States in 2015. The researchers found that three-quarters (72 percent) of the doctors had publicly identifiable Facebook pages, and 40 percent of those pages included "unprofessional or potentially objectionable" content. The content that was deemed unprofessional or potentially objectionable in the study ranged from profanity and images of drunkenness to clear violations of medical ethics, such as the discussion of patient health information.

The study found several cases where patient information was being posted. In one instance, a doctor posted X-rays that clearly displayed the patient's name. Other doctors disclosed enough information about a case for the patient to be identified, including describing specific complications during a surgery.

The researchers concluded that some doctors use social media in ways that could compromise their patients' trust in them.

Still other doctors, while they didn't disclose information, posted images of themselves at parties surrounded by alcohol, stating overly expressive political and religious opinions, and posting on other controversial lifestyle and social issues. This raises two questions: Should doctors accept friend requests from patients? Considering their trusted position, should doctors post public opinions that are unrelated to medicine?

We cannot expect doctors to post only content that is perfectly legal. However, we can take note of how we might feel if we see these behaviors from our doctors and apply that to how we manage our own online presences. The truth is that as long as you are not doing something illegal, if you have enough clout and your message is clear enough, you don't have to play by all the rules.

POTENTIALLY HARMFUL POSTS AND HOW TO AVOID THEM

Aside from patient information and the obvious drunken pictures of yourself on social media, what other types of posts are harmful? Accidentally posting or sharing fake news or misinformation is a big mistake. These are the types of posts that can make you lose credibility with your audience. Before you post, double-check the facts of the content. This can be done quite easily. If you are thinking, "I never share fake news," trust me, it can happen to anyone, and it happens more often than you know.

In 2016, the *Washington Post* published an article describing a study conducted by a group of computer scientists from Columbia University and the French National Institute to measure the percentage of shares on social media that people had not read before posting.[14] The study found that 59 percent of the links shared on social media had never actually been read before sharing. The study went a bit further, in that the scientists collected two other sets of data to be sure they were correct. They collected all of the Bit.ly (link shorteners) to five major news sources during a one-month period. Then they collected the number of clicks that were logged into Bit.ly's analytics to create a map of how news goes viral.

The researchers concluded that news does go viral but that it is not actually read. However, they also found that most of the clicks on viral news stories were links shared by Twitter users and not by the news outlets themselves. In other words, people are more likely to click a link and read an article if someone they follow has shared it. Since your followers will read what you publish more often than if it were published by an online news site, sharing fake news has a greater negative impact when shared by you—the person with a personal brand.

What does this mean? It means that nearly 60 percent of all links shared on Facebook and Twitter have never been viewed. Think of all of the wasted hours spent by people everywhere just trying to get posts out. When critics say that no one cares what you post online, what they mean is that if you don't care, why would anyone else?

The lesson is that there is no need to share a bunch of links you don't even read yourself. For those of you who do share links that you have not clicked on, beware: the link shorteners used on social media to track the reach of links have also been used to spread fake news by pretending the content has come from a news organization. A prime example of this is what happened during the 2016 presidential campaign, when a parody website called ABCNews. com.co pretended to be ABCNews.com. The site spread a lot of false information about the election, and no one realized that it was not coming from ABC News.

FOR HELP WITH FACT CHECKING

Here are a few websites that can help you check your facts and get more tips on how to avoid sharing nonsense:

whois.net
This website allows you to check who owns a website and can prevent you from sharing fake ABC News information (or from paying for fake Airbnb rentals).

continued

google.com Image Search
If you want to check where an image has originated from or where it has traveled, you can right-click the image and then click "Search Google for Image." If it is a new image, only a few links will appear; if it is old, several links will appear, and it is most likely spam.

factcheck.org
This nonpartisan, nonprofit project of the Annenberg Public Policy Center at the University of Pennsylvania monitors the factual accuracy of what is said by US political players, including politicians, TV ads, debates, interviews, and news releases. They also have a political literacy website (flackcheck.org) and other useful tools.

snopes.com
This site will help debunk the vast majority of urban legends, trending topics and images, and rumors spanning a huge number of topics.

truthorfiction.com
This website debunks all of the rumors that end up as memes or in chain emails. The site has mainstream information, but you can make requests as well.

projects.propublica.org/politwoops
This website lists all deleted tweets from sitting political officials and candidates. If you have a question about a tweet and you can't find it on this site, it probably never happened.

ANYONE AND EVERYONE CAN BE SCAMMED

I once threw my fiancé a birthday party and rented a house through a fake Airbnb site that was a copy of the real one. (When Airbnb tells you not to leave their website, they mean it.) I had booked a house for twenty-six people to stay overnight. My fiancé's birthday coincides with Halloween, and most of the people attending were coming in from out of town, so I made sure to book in advance. I was traveling for work and very busy, when I received an alert one day that said my Airbnb rental had been canceled by the host. When I messaged the host, he said that his phone application was giving him trouble and gave me his email. When I emailed him, he said that his wife was unfamiliar with the application and had accidentally cancelled my reservation. He apologized and sent me a link to get a discount for my troubles—a link to his fake Airbnb website. I paid the fee and went on my way. The day before the party, my bank called to say that they were unable to process the transaction. I emailed the host and asked him what was going on, and he told me that he wasn't sure but he would call Airbnb to find out. I didn't worry about it; I was just relieved that he was handling it. A few minutes later, I got another email from the host: "Airbnb says that the fastest way to get the money to me is for you to Western Union it." It was a hoax! I had less than twenty-four hours to find a new place in Los Angeles on Halloween week-end for twenty-six people. After hours of additional research and spending more money than I wanted to, I was able to secure a bona fide rental house to celebrate the occasion. I can't emphasize enough how important it is for you, your brand, and your audience to double-check every source.

7 PERCEPTION IS REALITY

When I asked for time off and left the country to work remotely for seven months, I sold everything I owned. When I returned to Los Angeles, I had two things to my name: my fifty-five-liter backpack with its contents and the job I had left behind. I had no home, no car, and no real belongings. But I also had a changed perspective and the drive to stay in Los Angeles and make it work. I temporarily moved in with my boyfriend, his brother, and their roommate. I would walk about six blocks to the train station every morning to ride downtown to my office. When I left my job for the day, I would stop in at the Macy's on the walk back to the train station and use my Macy's credit card to buy clothes for the next workday. I was absolutely broke, but my soul had never felt so free.

After a few weeks, I found a place of my own. Well, not exactly. I moved into an apartment with two men who lived in a three-bedroom in East Los Angeles. I was certain that the apartment was going to be amazing and a sign that my world was finally coming together. When I moved in, the roommate who happened to be the one I liked was moving out. I was concerned because the man who remained in the apartment seemed a little odd. I chose to ignore my intuition because, well, I really needed a place to live.

I stayed there for about one more week, until I realized that I had moved into an apartment with an insane person, one who counted squares of toilet paper, had a closet full of leather suits, and smoked cigarettes in his room with the AC on full-blast. I was so freaked out by him and his habits that I paid rent for the six months that I had agreed to live there and just left to live somewhere else. The only new place I could afford was way out in Pasadena. That was fine while I was working downtown, where the light-rail was located. A couple of months later, right after the holidays (and right after my twenty-sixth birthday), I was laid off along with the rest of my fellow employees. I needed a new a job, and fast.

Lucky for me, someone I went to high school with but had not seen since I was seventeen saw my post on Facebook about needing a job and responded. He said that he worked for a small SEO firm in Santa Monica that was hiring for what I had been doing: social media. I went in for the interview and immediately got the job. Unbelievably, my last day at my previous company was my first day at the new one.

Everything was going well, except that I lived in Pasadena, didn't have a car, and had just accepted a job in Santa Monica. The commute involves five freeways and a two- to two-and-a-half-hour drive each way, depending on traffic. (My own grandmother stopped answering my calls on my way to work because she didn't have two-plus hours to spend talking with me.)

My mission was to obtain a car. I heard that Volkswagen was offering a Jetta for zero down and $199 per month. It included maintenance and promised great gas mileage, so I was (pre)sold. I knew that if I went into the dealership, it would be a time drain, and if I called into the dealership, I would get so irritated by all the waiting that I would end up giving in without a negotiation to whatever they presented me.

But I had a plan. I was going to email every Volkswagen dealership in Los Angeles until one of them gave me exactly what I wanted: a 2012 black Jetta for zero down and $199 per month with my average to less-than-desirable credit.

I mass-emailed several dealerships in Los Angeles and the surrounding areas. My strategy was simple: minimize phone conversations and never give in. With the remaining days on the job I had just been laid off from, I started my search for a car. (The company paid all of us a severance to stay two weeks after the layoffs to help our users collect their content from the website.) I received email after email, followed up on my phone calls, and never gave up. I finally got a dealership to run my credit without my having to get on the phone. They got back to me and said they could go $2,000 down and $250 per month. I said, "No, thank you." They continued to call me, but I never answered. I emailed again and said that I wanted zero down and $199 per month. What did I have to lose? I could tell by the number of dealerships responding that they wanted the business, so I kept going.

The dealership that ran my credit came back with, "The best we can do is $500 down and $199 per month." I replied, "No problem, I will find someone who can help me." They tried to call but I didn't answer, and then they emailed me and said, "Okay, we got it approved. A 2012 Jetta for zero down and $199 per month." In that same email they wrote, "We have it in white or red; which one do you want?" I emailed them back with a simple reply: "Black."

The dealer was clearly becoming irritated, after I refused to answer his calls, when he emailed "We don't have it in black." I responded, "Then I will find someone else who can help me." A few hours went by, and he emailed me again to say, "Good news: we have the car in black, and we are having it brought over from another dealership for you now. When can you come in to get your car?"

I was excited, until I realized that I had found a dealership that was very far away. (This was before Uber was mainstream, and, remember, I was broke.) I emailed the dealer, "That's great news about the car! Unfortunately, I won't be able to come get it because I don't have a car. Do you offer any other solutions?" The salesman wrote, "No problem, Ms. Johnson, we will have the car driven to you, and you can sign your lease at that time."

The salesman delivered the car. When he met me he said, "You're Cynthia?" He had to meet the girl who was too busy to answer the phone. I laughed as I signed the lease on the hood of the car. And that is how I got my first car when I returned from traveling.

After two years with the car, I hit a pole while trying to park. (I am not the best driver—I'm definitely ready for autonomous vehicles.) When I took the car in for repairs, they told me it would be twenty-four hundred dollars to fix—more than I had paid for the car over the entire year. So I said, "No way," called the dealer I had leased the car from, and said, "I made a mistake with this one; may I have a new one?"

The dealer told me that he could fix it in-house to give me a better deal. When he pulled up my lease, he looked at me and said, "Who gave you such a good deal?" "You did," I replied. After I reminded him of who I was (yes, I thought I would be far more memorable, too), a lightbulb went on, and he remembered. Then I got another amazing deal, mainly because he expected me to negotiate one. His perception was that I would haggle with him, but in reality I was at the top of my negotiating game only when engaging via email.

Why was it so easy for me to get the deal I wanted the first time I tried? I carried out the entire deal within the confines of email. I didn't allow any personal bias to enter into the deal. (I even used an AOL email address.) The fact that I was aggressive, determined, and had injected nothing into my communication that would allude to my personality put me in control of the conversation. He was basically negotiating with an upset Yelp reviewer who had yet to leave a review.

Why did I get such a good deal the second time around? I had already established that I was able to negotiate. Negotiating takes time. When I went in to get my car, it was later in the day, and the dealer was in a rush to be somewhere else. His perception of the situation was that I would negotiate, take up his valuable time, and keep him there all night. So he skipped the negotiations, and I didn't have to do as much work the second time around.

What does this have to do with your personal brand? Perception can only be used in your favor when you know how most people perceive you. We all have qualities and identifiers that lead to preconceptions about who we are. Fully understanding those qualities and identifiers and how they change over time is important. There will always be situations where our individual attributes will be an advantage or a disadvantage.

There are also variations in others' perceptions of you. There is the way that people who know you perceive you, the way you perceive yourself, and the way your online presence is perceived. In most cases, your online presence reflects the way strangers perceive you as well.

Offline

To understand how people who know you actually perceive you, just ask them. Pick five close family members and friends to choose the descriptors that describe you. But before you do this, complete the exercise yourself so you can compare the way you see yourself with how they see you.

1.

    A.   Mostly conservative and traditional

    B.   Moderately conservative and traditional

    C.   Neutral

    D.   Moderately liberal and artistic

    E.   Liberal and artistic

2.

    A.   Mostly impulsive and spontaneous

    B.   Moderately impulsive and spontaneous

    C.   Neutral

D. Moderately organized and hardworking

E. Organized and hardworking

3.

A. Mostly contemplative

B. Moderately contemplative

C. Neutral

D. Moderately engaged with the outside world

E. Mostly engaged with the outside world

4.

A. Mostly competitive

B. Moderately competitive

C. Neutral

D. Moderately team working and trusting

E. Mostly team working and trusting

5.

A. Mostly laid-back and relaxed

B. Moderately laid-back and relaxed

C. Neutral

D. Moderately easily stressed and emotional

E. Mostly easily stressed and emotional

Give yourself one point for all A answers, two points for all B answers, three points for all C answers, four points for all D answers, and five points for all E answers.

For each question, create a sliding scale. If you received three B answers and two E answers for question 1, you would add 2 + 2 + 2 + 5 + 5 = 16 and then divide by 5, which would give you 3.2 or 32 percent.

0%	32%	100%
CONSERVATIVE·TRADITIONAL	YOU	LIBERAL·ARTISTIC

This range is to give you an idea of how the average person perceives you. You can segment this survey by asking five coworkers or colleagues, five family members, and five friends. Then compare the results based on how the respondents know you.

Online

Researchers Wu Youyou and David Stillwell from the Department of Psychology at the University of Cambridge and Michal Kosinski from the Department of Computer Science at Stanford University released a study declaring that "computer-based personality judgments are more accurate than those made by humans."[15] The researchers found that computers can judge your personality traits better than friends, family, and partners can. Using a new algorithm, researchers can use your Facebook likes, posts, and engagement metrics and your Twitter posts and engagement metrics to draw personality inferences about you that are as accurate as your parents' or partner's perceptions—and sometimes more accurate.

For their study, the researchers had 86,220 volunteers on Facebook complete a personality test that included one hundred questions. The volunteers also provided access to their Facebook likes. The personality test was used to provide self-reported personality scores for what psychologists call the Big Five traits: openness, conscientiousness, extroversion, agreeableness, and neuroticism. Then they compared the results to the volunteers' Facebook likes to create the algorithm that can form a perception of the person based on their online activity.

According to Stillwell, "The ability to judge personality is an essential component of social living—from day-to-day decisions to long-term plans such as whom to marry, trust, hire, or elect as president. The results of such data analysis can be very useful in aiding people when making decisions."

Coauthor Youyou added, "Recruiters could better match candidates with jobs based on their personality; products and services could adjust their behavior to best match their users' characters and changing moods. People may choose to augment their own intuitions and judgments with this kind of data analysis when making important life decisions such as choosing activities, career paths, or even romantic partners. Such data-driven decisions may well improve people's lives."

The good news? You can take the test (read on) and have your personality assessed online with the same tools used in the study.

The even-better news? If you know how you are being perceived both online and offline based on your likes, you can change the direction for your benefit. If you want that promotion or job opportunity, you can compare yourself to people who have those opportunities coming to them and adjust accordingly, just as you would tailor your résumé.

People may say that manipulating your personality online to achieve your goals is not an authentic approach. But consider the ways we are already doing this. We don't approach dating the same way we approach a job interview. If our online presence is being used to assess our ability to do a job, then we have every incentive to adjust accordingly. In doing so, you are showing the kind of attention to detail that is expected by anyone who wants to hire or collaborate.

For example, I know that I have reached my personal goals on Facebook when I see ads for executive training programs and corporate lawyers.

THE TEST

Now you get to take the test yourself. Below are the links to the tests and research. In some cases, I have used link shorteners for the links that are very long. (Remember, link shorteners are case sensitive, so always use lowercase for the links in this book.)

» mypersonality.org: This is information on the research and updates.

» applymagicsauce.com: This is where you can connect your Twitter account to have their algorithm predict your personality.

» discovermyprofile.com: This is where you can find additional questionnaires and tests that you can complete to discover your psychological profile.

My results follow (Remember, I manipulate my results by choosing not to post personal content.)

I am thirty, but my online behavior is that of a thirty-three-year-old . . . according to the internet.

Age

33

Your digital footprint suggests that your online behaviour resembles that of a 30-39 year old

My psychological gender suggests that I am the "epitome of masculinity."

Psychological Gender ❶

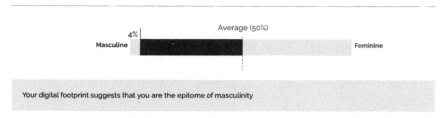

My personality

Big 5 Personality ❶ (Predictions are expressed as percentiles)

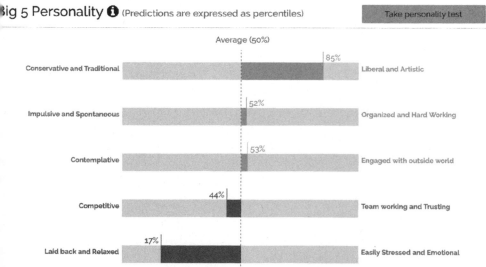

MY JUNGIAN PERSONALITY TYPE (MYERS-BRIGGS®) ASSESSMENT): ENTJ

According to Myers-Briggs, ENTJ stands for Extroverted + iNtuitive + Thinking + Judging. ENTJs often excel in business. They are assertive, outspoken, confident, outgoing, energetic, charismatic, fair-minded, and unaffected by conflict or criticism. However, other traits may lessen the impact of their strengths. They may appear argumentative, confrontational, insensitive, intimidating, and controlling. They can overwhelm others with their energy, intelligence, and desire to order the world around them.

ENTJs tend to cultivate their personal power and often end up taking charge of a situation that seems (in their mind, at least) to be out of control. Also, ENTJs seek knowledge and strive to learn new things, which helps them become good problem solvers. They may be viewed by others as aloof and coldhearted, since ENTJs appear to take a tough approach to emotional or personal issues. In situations requiring feeling and value judgments, ENTJs are well served to seek the advice of a trusted Feeling type.

There are some truths here, and some results that are manipulated. But if you want to rebrand, these results are important in understanding your preferences.

OPEN TEXT PREDICTION

If you are looking for help in identifying your personality profile goals or to see how else you can be perceived, this tool also allows you to upload text with no minimum word count; however, at least two hundred words is preferred.

To give an example, I uploaded a paragraph from this book to see how I was perceived as the author. The results were that I was mostly female (transparent conversation versus the managed persona on Facebook) and that I was forty-eight years old (high-level conversation versus Facebook posts). My personality type even changed from ENTJ (Extroverted + iNtuitive + Thinking + Judging) to INTJ (Introverted + iNtuitive + Thinking + Judging).

INTJs are very analytical individuals. They are more comfortable working alone than with other people, and are not usually as sociable as others, although they are prepared to take the lead if nobody else is up to the task, or they see a major weakness in the current leadership. They tend to be very pragmatic and logical individuals, often with an individualistic bent and a low tolerance for spin or rampant emotionalism. They are also generally not susceptible to catchphrases and commonly do not recognize authority based on tradition, rank, or title. Hallmark features of the INTJ personality type include independence of thought, strong individualism, and creativity.

Persons with this personality type work best given large amounts of autonomy and creative freedom. They harbor an innate desire to express themselves; that is, they want to be creative by conceptualizing their own intellectual designs. Analyzing and formulating complex theories are among their greatest strengths.

This description is a much better fit for the book I am writing. You can change the way the internet and algorithms perceive you, just as you would behave differently in front of your mom than you would at a job interview. You get to decide how you are perceived. Now run your own tests to gather information on how you are perceived, because perception is reality.

CASE STUDY: PERCEPTION IN PRACTICE AND THE CASE FOR MAINTAINING IT

A study published in January 2017 assessed the student evaluations of teaching (SET), or student reviews of teachers, which are widely used in academic personnel decision making as a measure of effectiveness.[16] This large-scale study of RateMyProfessors.com data looked for correlations, trends, and potential biases in publicly accessible web-based student evaluations of teaching. The study sourced 7,882,980 reviews (of 190,006 US professors with at least twenty student ratings) to provide insight into student perceptions of academic instruction and possible variables in student evaluations.

The study found that women did not have higher scores than men in any of the fields, but some difficult fields (such as chemistry) showed no difference in ratings between the two. Professors who taught science, technology, engineering, and math had lower scores than those who taught humanities and arts. Professors who had classes that were rated as easy had better overall scores. This study specifically left out professors who were considered "hot" because they had better ratings. Go figure.

The author of this study, Andrew S. Rosen, a PhD candidate in chemical engineering at Northwestern University, told InsideHighered.com how he felt about the results of the study: "Even if critics shrug at data from [RateMyProfessors], the biases present on the site are of particular importance," because they imply that potentially invalid metrics exist in institutional evaluations as well. He added, "They still have significant importance in both the course selection process for students and the academic promotion process. I don't anticipate this will change anytime soon, so studies like this can highlight ways institutional [evaluations of teaching] can be more critically and accurately evaluated."

Perception: Professors who teach easier courses are better teachers.

Reality: Some course subjects are easier than other subjects.

Perception: Professors who have better ratings are better at their jobs and deserve more promotions than teachers with worse ratings.

Reality: Professors who teach less-complicated subjects get better ratings.

IMPOSTOR SYNDROME IS HURTING OUR WORLD

In my career, I have been in situations where I was the right person for the job but felt as if I weren't, and I have been in situations where I was definitely the wrong person for the situation I was placed in.

Imposter syndrome runs rampant among high achievers and doers. These are people who have more experience, knowledge, and education than some of us could ever imagine. Yet they attribute most of their success to luck. They brush off the compliments and excitement over their achievements by saying things like, "Anyone could have done it," or, "I just got lucky." Imposter syndrome is a fear that all of your success is based on luck or that someone else's poor judgment is what led to your opportunity.

Imposter syndrome is hurting the world. It is hurting our economy, education system, political system, and corporations. When the right people for the job are humble and, in an effort to seem modest, leave out the most successful parts of their story for fear of being judged, then the best are shying away from attention while the unqualified are ending up in positions of decision-making authority.

The first time you are put into a new situation, you may run the risk of failure. The thing to remember is, *so does everyone else.* We are all just trying to figure it out. All of us. How do you get past those fears? Assert your excellence. One reason the world is off-kilter is that there aren't enough people competing at a high level. Are people challenging one another at high levels? Sure. Is everyone who could compete actually competing? Nope.

How do you make sure people know what you want them to know that you know without feeling as if you are bragging? Show; don't tell. Here's how:

» Make sure your LinkedIn profile is complete. Whenever you add a positive update, make sure you have "Share changes with your audience" turned on so that your followers will see what you added.

» If you get media attention, a new job, or anything else that you wish people could see but you don't want to seem full of yourself, send it to your mom, partner, sibling, or someone else that you have a close relationship with. Once they have posted it and gloated about you, you can acknowledge it, everyone will see it, and your mom (or whoever) looks like a superhero.

» Don't talk about what you can *do*; instead, show what you have *done*. Avoid too much commentary on or explanation of your success. People want to congratulate you, so let them and do the same in return.

» Make sure people can contact you (or your branded self).

» Put your email and other contact information on your profile and website. Make sure people know how they can contact you and what they should contact you about.

» Create a media email address (Media@YourWebsite.com, or whatever) if you don't have an assistant or agent (as most of us don't). Be your own helper. That way you can negotiate on your own behalf while keeping impostor syndrome at bay.

ARE WE LIVING IN A MATRIX?

I think we might be living in a Matrix (or what we now call a computer simulation). We are probably connected to a simulator that tells our brains stories, like virtual reality, but it is our own reality. Personal branding is really just a game inside the game. How did we get here? Who controls it? Aliens, most likely.

Before you continue reading, please ask yourself, *Do I believe Cynthia when she says that we are most likely living in a Matrix?* Register your answer and continue reading.

Do you think I am crazy? Or do you see what I see? Have you ever heard of Moore's law? It basically claims that computers double in size every year. This means that supercomputers have the ability to compute the entire eighty-year life span of a human being in a decade. That would include every single thought, dream, and declaration. So it is entirely possible that we are living in a Matrix, right?

Don't believe me? What if I told you that NASA, Elon Musk, and Bank of America Merrill Lynch have all publicly acknowledged that we are probably living in a Matrix?

The philosophy was first introduced by Swedish philosopher Nick Bostrom, a young scientist with a lot of original ideas. Dr. Bostrom believes that descendants who are much more evolved than we are could have us imprisoned in a digital world.

In an interview with VICE, Rich Terrile, director of the Center for Evolutionary Computation and Automated Design at NASA's Jet Propulsion Laboratory talked openly about NASA's supercomputers and how they are computing at twice the speed of the average human brain:

> "In quantum mechanics, particles do not have a definite state unless they're being observed. Many theorists have spent a lot of time trying to figure out how you explain this. One explanation is that we're living within a simulation, seeing what we need to see when we need to see it. What I find inspiring is that, even if we are in a simulation or many orders of magnitude down in levels of simulation, somewhere along the line something escaped the primordial ooze to become us and to result in simulations that made us—and that's cool."

According to Terrile, "the idea that our universe is a fiction generated by computer code solves a number of inconsistencies and mysteries about the cosmos."

Before you continue reading, ask yourself again whether you believe me now. Register your answer and then continue reading.

In 2016, analysts from Bank of America Merrill Lynch sent out a report about virtual reality to their clients. The report stated, "It is conceivable that with advancements in artificial intelligence, virtual reality, and computing power, members of future civilizations could have decided to run a simulation of their ancestors."

According to an article in *Business Insider*, the Bank of America report explained that "many scientists, philosophers, and business leaders believe that there is a 20 to 50 percent probability that humans are already living in a computer-simulated virtual world. In April 2016, researchers gathered at the American Museum of Natural History to debate this notion. The argument is that we are already approaching photorealistic 3D simulations that millions of people can simultaneously participate in."

Before you continue reading, ask yourself, *Do I believe Cynthia even more now?* Register your answer and continue reading. (I'm starting to sound like a simulation myself.)

Still not convinced? Well Elon Musk also believes that we are living in a Matrix or simulation. Here are his words from the Code Conference in 2016:

> "The strongest argument for us probably being in a simulation I think is the following. Forty years ago we had Pong—two rectangles and a dot. That's where we were. Now, forty years later, we have photorealistic, 3D simulations with millions of people playing simultaneously, and it's getting better every year. And soon we'll have virtual reality; we'll have augmented reality. If you assume any rate of improvement at all, then the games will become indistinguishable from reality, just indistinguishable, and because we will not be able to distinguish real from unreal, it would seem to follow that the odds that we're in 'base reality' is one in billions. Otherwise, if civilization stops advancing, then that may be due to some calamitous event that stops civilization."

Apparently, some as-yet unnamed tech billionaires believe the theory so much that they have actually hired scientists to try to help us escape.

Now, one last time: do you believe me more now than you did at the beginning of this section—that there is a possibility that we might be living in a Matrix?

You may not believe me more or less, but you definitely understand how I could come to that conclusion after hearing all the other people who have agreed on the possibility. We perceive the relevance and likelihood of an idea by first judging the reliability of the source.

When ordinary people claim they believe in or have seen aliens, they are often considered crazy and may be exiled by family, friends, and society. However, when Elon Musk and NASA say they believe, then we start to believe with them.

We also tend to believe people and companies who state outrageous ideas when we know they have something to lose. For example, we will take more time in considering whether we are living in a Matrix if Bank of America Merrill Lynch says we are—especially if they tell it to their clients. Why? We believe them more because there is an obvious risk for them to say this. They could lose a majority of their clients, if not all of them. So they must be telling the truth; otherwise, why would they take such a risk?

This is an example of a great way to spread your ideas: have the least likely source spread them for you. Convincing one person or company is easier than trying to convince the world. If I hadn't heard that Bank of America Merrill Lynch told their clients about their report suggesting that we are already living in a Matrix, I never would have believed it. I still don't believe it, but after hearing that, I have genuinely considered it.

Some of you may have started to consider it, too, after reading about the spread of this idea by sources we perceive as credible who have no incentive to perpetuate it. This is how we shift mindsets and start rumors. The theory was first written four years after the movie *The Matrix* was released. Did the film inspire the scientific research? Maybe. We are all subconsciously inspired by what we read, hear, and see. That is the power of branding.

HOW EFFECTIVE COMMUNICATION CAN DISTRACT FROM THE TRUTH

Building a brand that benefits you and your mission has little to do with you personally. It has everything to do with how people feel about you and how you make people feel. One of the best examples of this is when we see people who want more followers but fail to offer a compelling reason to follow them. This is similar to asking for money without ever completing the job. Someone might give it to them once but never again if the work is not completed. The term *personal branding* sounds like "It's all about me," but when an individual is good at it, the value can be even greater for the brand adopter than for the brand creator.

There is always a gatekeeper who regulates personal branding, influence, career development, politics, and everything similar. These are the people we have to persuade and connect with in order to move on to bigger and better opportunities. This requires that we understand what these people or their audiences need and provide it for them. How is this done?

The first thing you need to have is a message. This is your mission, your goal, your purpose. This mission can and will change, but that is okay. You have to start somewhere, and you can always pivot at a later point. Your mission can be as expansive as "To save the world" or as narrow as "To have a happy and healthy family."

CASE STUDY: ELON MUSK AND TRAVIS KALANICK

Elon Musk is possibly the most interesting and successful case study in personal branding since the Rockefellers. He has shown us how an individual can directly impact the rise and fall of stock for a billion-dollar corporation. One of the highest profile stocks in recent years is that of Tesla, the electric automotive and energy storage company Musk founded in 2003. This company has surpassed Ford's market value despite ongoing annual losses. Tesla's stock has long been closely tied to Elon Musk's brand, which portrays him as the enigmatic genius and forward-thinking CEO.

Always thinking bigger and better, Musk has become synonymous with the socially conscious, mad-genius persona who has driven all three of his companies to new heights. In fact, it's so pronounced that when Elon Musk posted this tweet in August 2016, Tesla's stock increased by 2 percent, adding $670 million to the company's value at the time. The mere mention of a new product, feature, or technology is enough to bring about a surge in the value of the stock.

Elon Musk ✔
@elonmusk

Tesla product announcement at noon California time today

8:23 AM - 23 Aug 2016

↩ ⟲ 5,168   ♥ 14,158

And it isn't just stocks that Elon has been able to sway. He has also become a crusader who is rarely questioned. In fact, we question ourselves before we question him. In December 2016, Elon Musk and Travis Kalanick (founder and former CEO of Uber) joined President Donald Trump's economic team. The headlines were filled with talk and opinions on the matter. Soon after, on January 27, 2017, the Trump administration issued the executive order banning US entry for ninety days by citizens of Iraq, Syria, Iran, Libya, Somalia, Sudan, and Yemen. The order also indefinitely halted refugees from Syria.

Internet communities were appalled, and #DeleteUber hashtags began trending, encouraging users to delete their Uber accounts and use Lyft instead. (It should be noted that Peter Thiel and Carl Icahn, both Trump supporters and advisors, own substantial stock in Lyft.) The pressure was intense for Uber and for Tesla as well.

I have created a distilled timeline of the events and media surrounding Travis Kalanick, Uber, Elon Musk, and Tesla from January 2017 through August 2017. This timeline was created to examine the actual events and media surrounding the two CEOs and their companies, without judgment or politicization. The objective is to compare and discuss the events as they were covered in the media, when they took place, and the responses from each CEO or his company spokesperson.

January 27, 2017: Both CEOs and their companies start to receive significant criticism because of their participation in the president's council in response to President Trump's immigration ban.

January 28, 2017: The Taxi Workers Alliance, a nonprofit union that represents drivers in New York City, stood outside of John F. Kennedy International Airport with protesters in opposition to the travel ban. The alliance asked its members to stop work at the airport between 6 p.m. and 7 p.m. At 7:36 p.m. (thirty minutes after the strike would have ended), Uber tweeted that it had turned off surge pricing at the airport.

January 28, 2017: Soon after the tweet, #DeleteUber started trending, and more than 500,000 users said they would delete their accounts. (The number of those who actually did is unclear, but the estimate is 200,000.)

January 28, 2017: Five people (the confirmed number is not reported) said they canceled the one thousand dollar deposits on their Tesla Model 3 orders.

January 29, 2017: Travis Kalanick went on Facebook and announced that Uber created a $3 million defense fund for drivers who are citizens of Iran, Syria, Iraq, Libya, Somalia, Sudan, and Yemen and who live in the United States but left the country and would not be able to return for ninety days. He and Uber recognized that this meant these people would not be able to work and would need compensation for lost earnings. He added a link to submit information for individuals, their friends, and family members who were affected.

January 29, 2017: Elon Musk went on Twitter to address the issue and the concerns of Tesla fans. He asked that people read the order and suggest amendments.

February 2, 2017: Travis Kalanick stepped down from Trump's economic team in response to consumer criticism. Elon Musk did not.

February 5, 2017: A host of big-name tech companies, including Apple, Facebook, Google, Twitter, and Microsoft, filed an amicus brief in a Washington state court opposing Donald Trump's executive order on immigration. Uber signed on. Tesla did not.

February 13, 2017: While attending the World Government Summit in Dubai, I was able to see two speakers back-to-back: Travis Kalanick followed by Elon Musk. Travis Kalanick ran through a SlideShare deck showing a lot of facts and data about driving. He was then interviewed onstage by a reporter from a large US news network, who appeared as though she had just been told that she was not allowed to ask about his former involvement with Donald Trump. The reporter ended the interview by asking Kalanick if he was aware of and prepared for the responsibility that his success had brought him. He answered. Then she walked offstage, leaving Kalanick to follow behind her.

February 13, 2017 (about an hour later): Elon Musk's interview went differently. (I should mention that Tesla was launching cars in the United Arab Emirates that weekend.) Musk did not provide a presentation; instead, he was interviewed question-and-answer style by a moderator in the UAE. At the end of the interview, the moderator dubbed him "the next Einstein." Musk then stood up and shook hands with the moderator before exiting the stage to loud applause. During that interview, he did not discuss how he planned to help the world, as Kalanick had done; instead, he said that he believed aliens were real, that tunnels could remove traffic, and that basic income would soon become necessary.

February 19, 2017: Susan Fowler, a former engineer at Uber, wrote in a blog post about her year working for the company. Her post contained detailed allegations about sexual harassment by her manager as well as the HR department's reluctance to take action. Her blog put the focus on the alleged rampant misogyny and the hostile work environment for female employees at Uber.

February 19, 2017: The Uber CEO released the following statement, "I have just read Susan Fowler's blog. What she describes is abhorrent and against everything Uber stands for and believes in. It's the first time this has come to my attention, so I have instructed Liane Hornsey, our new chief human resources officer, to conduct an urgent investigation into these allegations. We seek to make Uber a just workplace, and there can be absolutely no place for this kind of behavior at Uber—and anyone who behaves this way or thinks this is OK will be fired."

February 20, 2017 (the next day): Uber hired two partners from the law firm Covington & Burling—former US attorney general Eric Holder and Tammy Albarran—to probe the sexual harassment claims. Uber appointed the company's general council and two women from the board to assist.

February 28, 2017: Uber asked senior executive Amit Singhal to leave the company for failing to disclose a sexual harassment allegation during his time at Google.

February 28, 2017: A female engineer who was still employed at Tesla reached out to the *Guardian* about her sexual harassment and gender discrimination lawsuit, filed against Tesla months earlier (in the fall of 2016).

February 28, 2017, to March 1, 2017: Travis Kalanick was caught on camera swearing at an Uber driver, who had asked the CEO about his management style and blamed him for undercutting the fares. Kalanick responded as he left the cab, "Some people don't like to take responsibility for their own shit. They blame everything in their life on somebody else. Good luck!" The video went viral, and Kalanick apologized in an email to his employees.

March 2, 2017: An auto writer for *InsideEVs* and *U.S. News & World Report*, who is the father of a fifth grader, tweeted a letter that his daughter wrote to Elon Musk about her marketing idea for Tesla.

Elon Musk responded, approving her marketing plan and putting it into action.

March 24, 2017: Gabi Holzwarth, Kalanick's former girlfriend, told the media that she was with Kalanick and a team of five Uber employees when they visited an escort-karaoke bar in Seoul in 2014. According to Holzwarth, women sat in a circle wearing tags with numbers on them. Four of the male employees, who were Uber managers, picked women by calling out their numbers. About an hour later, she, Kalanick, and the female Uber employee left.

April 3, 2017: Tesla's market cap surpassed Ford's at $53 billion.[17] According to The Verge, in 2016, Tesla—which lost $675 million on $7 billion in revenue—was worth more than GM (with revenue of $166.4 billion and net income of $9.43 billion) and Ford (with sales of $151.8 billion and net income of $4.6 billion).

April 19, 2017: Three Tesla drivers filed a lawsuit in the US District Court in San Jose, California, alleging that the company knowingly sold them vehicles with "enhanced autopilot" technology that was unsafe.

April 24, 2017: Uber was hit with a lawsuit for using a secret software program (internally referred to as "hell") to track Lyft drivers. The technology allegedly enabled Uber to see how many Lyft drivers were in an area and how much they were charging.

May 18, 2017: Employees from the Tesla factory told the *Guardian* of the negative work environment, citing grueling pressure and even life-altering injuries. They attributed these hazards to Musk's aggressive production goals. The article stated that "ambulances have been called more than 100 times since 2014 for workers experiencing fainting spells, dizziness, seizures, abnormal breathing, and chest pains, according to incident reports obtained by the *Guardian*. Hundreds more were called for injuries and other medical issues."

May 23, 2017: Uber admitted to underpaying drivers in New York City by taking a higher percentage of the fare than they had agreed to do. The company was ordered to pay $900 million to its drivers.

Uber's formal agreement with drivers is for the company to keep between 20 and 25 percent of the fare after deducting sales tax and a local fee for a fund to benefit injured drivers. Instead, Uber was basing its percentage on the gross fare.

May 27, 2017: Travis Kalanick's mother, Bonnie Kalanick, died in a boating accident.

June 1, 2017: Tesla fired AJ Vandermeyden, the woman who had filed a sexual harassment and gender discrimination lawsuit against the company in August 2016. Tesla's representative stated, "Despite repeatedly receiving special treatment at the expense of others, Ms. Vandermeyden nonetheless chose to pursue a miscarriage of justice by suing Tesla and falsely attacking our company in the press. . . . The termination was based on Ms. Vandermeyden behaving in what the evidence indicates is a fundamentally false and misleading manner, not as a result of retaliation for the lawsuit."

June 2, 2017: Elon Musk and Disney's Bob Iger left Trump's advisory council after the United States exited the Paris climate deal.

June 6, 2017: Uber fired more than twenty employees as a result of the sexual harassment and company culture probe.

June 7, 2017: Information leaks alleged that a top Uber executive, Eric Alexander, had obtained the medical records of a woman raped by an Uber driver, to cast doubt on the victim's report. Alexander was fired only after journalists learned of the incident, according to tech website Recode and the *New York Times*.

June 13, 2017: Travis Kalanick took an indefinite leave of absence, stating in an email to staff, "I need to take some time off of the day-to-day to grieve my mother, whom I buried on Friday, to reflect, to work on myself, and to focus on building out a world-class leadership team. If we are going to work on Uber 2.0, I also need to work on Travis 2.0 to become the leader that this company needs and that you deserve."

June 21, 2017: Under pressure from five of Uber's investors, Travis Kalanick permanently stepped down as CEO of Uber.

July 6, 2017: Tesla registrations plunged 24 percent in California, its largest market. An article in *ZeroHedge* stated, "Tesla declined to comment on California registration figures and reverted back to its Monday's press release that second-quarter global deliveries rose 53 percent from a year earlier, to just over 12,000 Model S and just over 10,000 Model X, which incidentally also missed consensus expectations of 22,900 sales."

August 7, 2017: Tesla launched its first high-yield junk bond offering at $1.8 billion, $300 million more than expected and at a yield of 5.25 percent, according to Inform Global Markets. According to CNBC, Tesla burned through $1.2 billion in the second quarter alone in the attempt to produce more cars. Larry McDonald, author of the *Bear Traps Report*, wrote, "It speaks to the sheer insanity found in the high yield market to have a deal like this upsized with terms so unappealing to investors. The deck is stacked for Tesla in bond deal terms; congrats to Elon Musk."

It is clear from this timeline of events that Elon Musk emerged from an exceedingly difficult period in much better shape than did Travis Kalanick—but why?

Let's take a look at the responses to the travel ban from each executive to get a clearer understanding of what transpired. The timeline shows that both CEOs received pushback after the travel ban for being on President Trump's advisory council. But we see two different kinds of responses: reactive and proactive.

Travis Kalanick's response was to create a $3 million legal defense fund to provide drivers with immigration and translation services, and then to post it on Facebook. Sounds like a good plan, right? But the problem with his response is that it is reactionary. He reacted to the fact that people were going to #DeleteUber, instead of responding to the source of this problem: the travel ban. In other words, he failed to address the reason people had gotten upset in the first place. He didn't apologize, take responsibility, or even acknowledge that the tweet had happened.

Travis Kalanick
January 29 · 🌐

Standing up for the driver community:

Here's the email I'm sending to drivers affected by President's unjust immigration and travel ban:

At Uber we've always believed in standing up for what's right. Today we need your help supporting drivers who may be impacted by the President's unjust immigration ban.

Drivers who are citizens of Iran, Iraq, Libya, Somalia, Sudan, Syria or Yemen and live in the US but have left the country, will not be able to return for 90 days. This means they won't be able to earn money and support their families during this period.

So it's important that as a community that we do everything we can to help these drivers. Here's what Uber will do:

- Provide 24/7 legal support for drivers who are trying to get back into the country. Our lawyers and immigration experts will be on call 24/7 to help.
- Compensate drivers for their lost earnings. This will help them support their families and put food on the table while they are banned from the US;
- Urge the government to reinstate the right of U.S. residents to travel - whatever their country of origin - immediately;
- Create a $3 million legal defense fund to help drivers with immigration and translation services.

If you are a driver or a friend or family member of someone who has been affected, please contact us at: https://goo.gl/forms/AlJTivooFxuExX1p1.

Uber is a community. We're here to support each other. Please help Uber to help drivers who may be affected by this wrong and unjust immigration ban.

-Travis

This is the kind of message that makes people feel like they might as well be talking to a wall. Personal branding, whether proactive (created and maintained before it is necessary) or reactive (created to dissolve a problem or save a reputation), has nothing to do with what you do for people or what you say about yourself and your company. It has everything to do with how you make people feel, how you engage with them, and what they say about you to your face and to others. Kalanick and Uber's response revealed a lack of understanding of the real issue.

From the media and public's perspective, Kalanick had never told them why he joined Trump's advisory council, so they drew their own conclusions. He never tweeted in support of the protests; instead, Uber used it as an excuse to draw more business with a tweet. When Kalanick faced the backlash, he responded by throwing money at the problem he perceived, not to the real one that had caused the protest. In the eyes of the crowd, he was a profit-focused CEO parading as a false martyr.

Elon Musk's response to the travel ban was slightly different. He did not wait for the backlash; instead, he tweeted his thoughts. He did not offer a solution; he responded to the people in a thread.

Elon Musk ✔ @elonmusk · Jan 28
The blanket entry ban on citizens from certain primarily Muslim countries is not the best way to address the country's challenges

   ◯ 2.7K   ⟲ 20K   ♡ 57K   ✉

Elon Musk ✔
@elonmusk

      (Follow)

Many people negatively affected by this policy are strong supporters of the US. They've done right,not wrong & don't deserve to be rejected.

4:35 PM - 28 Jan 2017

13,382 Retweets **40,957** Likes

◯ 1.2K   ⟲ 13K   ♡ 41K   ✉

The next day, he sent another tweet asking people to read the executive order and give him feedback so that he could take their advice to the president and seek the advisory council's consensus. This tweet accomplished two things. First, asking people why they were upset and asking them for the specifics showed that he was listening. Second, his response put him in a position to help make a change. It gave the people an advocate inside the White House. Suddenly, it made sense why Elon Musk was at the president's table—to create change from within the establishment.

Elon Musk ✓ @elonmusk · Jan 29

Please read immigration order. Lmk specific amendments. Will seek advisory council consensus & present to President.

Text of Trump Executive Order on Barring Refugees
Here is the text of the executive order by President Donald Trump that indefinitely bans Syrian refugees from entering the U.S. and puts a four-...
blogs.wsj.com

💬 3.1K   ⟲ 3.9K   ♡ 10K   ✉

Elon Musk is very proactive with his brand. He has one mission in life, and that is "To save the world." He can join Trump's economic team because he is trying to save the world. He can dig tunnels, launch rockets, and talk about autonomous vehicles and guaranteed minimum income. He can do all of these things because at the end of the day they fit with his personal brand: the guy who is trying to save the world. People can clearly see what he is about, and this leads to forgiveness. When Elon Musk does something that seems questionable, people will stop and ask themselves what they've missed, trusting that since Musk is always focused on saving the world, he must be doing so now.

Kalanick quit Trump's economic team in response to the negative feedback, but Musk did not. In theory, Kalanick and Uber should have looked like superstars for signing the amicus brief in a Washington state court, opposing President Trump's executive order on immigration. Another thing Kalanick did that Musk did not do was to negotiate. Kalanick joined the team, then condemned the team, then seemingly broke up the protest to make money, then wanted to give money away, and then quit the advisory council, leaving everyone to conclude they had no idea of Kalanick's true intentions. This demonstrates how people with influence can give in to pressure in order to avoid conflict, yet end up appearing disconnected from the problem—and from their audience.

Kalanick immediately addressed the claim that Uber had a sexist culture. He brought people on board to help, hired a top-notch consulting firm, fired an executive, and launched a full-scale probe into the allegations. Let's look at the words that ultimately made his statement ineffective:

> "I have just read Susan Fowler's blog. What she describes is abhorrent and against everything Uber stands for and believes in. It's the first time this has come to my attention so I have instructed Liane Hornsey, our new chief human resources officer, to conduct an urgent investigation into these allegations. We seek to make Uber a just workplace and there can be absolutely no place for this kind of behavior at Uber—and anyone who behaves this way or thinks this is OK will be fired."

The use of the word *I* instead of *we* appears egocentric, while the use of *Uber* instead of *we* is not inclusive. The claim that this is the first time Kalanick had heard about the issue may seem false to many because he has not established trust in how he treats others and how others feel about him. The investigation and threat to fire current employees suggests that the CEO trusts the former employee's statement more than he trusts the people who currently work for him.

Musk and Tesla had a different approach to the lawsuit for sexual harassment and discrimination. In the statement Tesla made to TechCrunch, I have highlighted what the company did right:

> "Tesla is committed to creating a positive workplace environment that is free of discrimination for all our employees. Ms. Vandermeyden joined Tesla in a sales position in 2013, and since then, despite having no formal engineering degree, she has sought and moved into successive engineering roles, beginning with her work in Tesla's paint shop and eventually another role in General Assembly. Even after she made her complaints of alleged discrimination, she sought and was advanced into at least one other new role, evidence of the fact that Tesla is committed to rewarding hard work and talent, regardless of background. When Ms. Vandermeyden first brought her concerns to us over a year ago, we immediately retained a neutral third party, Anne Hilbert of EMC2Law, to investigate her claims so that, if warranted, we could take appropriate action to address the issues she raised. After an exhaustive review of the facts, the independent investigator determined that Ms. Vandermeyden's 'claims of gender discrimination, harassment, and retaliation have not been substantiated.' Without this context, the story presented in the original article is misleading."

Notice that the word *free* (of discrimination) is used here, instead of *against* or similar oppositional words. *Our employees* signifies unity within the company. The employee's story was told in its entirety, from the moment she was hired to the present. Tesla admits to having heard her complaints and explains the action that was taken. Instead of deciding on an action immediately, Tesla brought in a neutral lawyer to investigate the employee's claims, so that if they turned out to be true, the necessary action could be taken. The employee's name is mentioned multiple times in the statement. The last line provides the full context, implying that the story would be inaccurate, incomplete, and misleading without it.

As Kalanick was caught screaming at an Uber driver who was complaining about the way Uber treats and pays drivers, Musk was taking marketing advice from a fifth-grader, proving once again that listening and genuinely responding is the wise approach. Later, Kalanick emailed the following message to his internal team and then republished it to his company blog:

"By now I'm sure you've seen the video where I treated an Uber driver disrespectfully. To say that I am ashamed is an extreme understatement. My job as your leader is to lead . . . and that starts with behaving in a way that makes us all proud. That is not what I did, and it cannot be explained away. It's clear this video is a reflection of me—and the criticism we've received is a stark reminder that I must fundamentally change as a leader and grow up. This is the first time I've been willing to admit that I need leadership help and I intend to get it. I want to profoundly apologize to Fawzi, as well as the driver and rider community, and to the Uber team."

In this memo to his team and to the world, Kalanick admits that he is wrong, that he does not know why he did what he did, and that he has failed as leader. The problem with this approach is that he has delivered the same message to two different entities, suggesting that it is not personal or genuine. It reminds me of the advice my younger brother once gave me about Snapchat. "Cynthia, don't add your snap to your story and then send me the same one," he said. "It doesn't make me feel special." My brother was right: individual snaps are like personal messages. They are only valuable to people when they are clearly for their eyes only.

A few days after Kalanick's rant to the Uber driver went viral, employees at a Tesla factory in Fremont, California, complained of a terrible work environment, injuries, and insane schedules. Following is the response from Elon Musk:

"No words can express how much I care about your safety and well-being. It breaks my heart when someone is injured building cars and trying their best to make Tesla successful. Going forward, I've asked that every injury be reported directly to me, without exception. I'm meeting with the safety team every week and would like to meet every injured person as soon as they are well, so that

I can understand from them exactly what we need to do to make it better. I will then go down to the production line and perform the same task that they perform. This is what all managers at Tesla should do as a matter of course. At Tesla, we lead from the front line, not from some safe and comfortable ivory tower. Managers must always put their team's safety above their own."

Elon Musk does not explain why the injuries happened, deny that they happened, or blame the employees. Instead, he assumes responsibility, creates a plan to meet with and listen to employees individually, offers to do their job so that he can see the issues first-hand, and places the responsibility on company managers to follow in his footsteps. His message reflects his core mission—"To save the world"—beginning with making sure that employees under-stand that he does not merely see them as numbers or problems but as individuals. Does he actually believe this? Who knows? But his brand leads us to believe he does.

Uber's response to underpaying their drivers was to email each driver. Below is a copy of the email that was posted in a *Recode* article:[18]

Dear   ,

We've identified that due to a discrepancy between your pay statements and our terms of service, you're owed $938.65.

We apologize. The issue has been fixed, and we have taken action to ensure that it does not happen again.

You will be receiving a one-time payment from Uber for the period between November 10, 2014 and May 21, 2017, plus interest. To make sure your payment is processed correctly, confirm your bank details are up-to-date at vault.uber.com.

We will deposit $938.65 into your bank account on file within 7 days.

Additionally, as of Monday, May 22, you'll notice an increase in earnings of 2-3% in NYC.

In contrast, here is Tesla's response to firing the female employee who claimed sexual harassment:

> "Despite repeatedly receiving special treatment at the expense of others, Ms. Vandermeyden nonetheless chose to pursue a miscarriage of justice by suing Tesla and falsely attacking our company in the press. After we carefully considered the facts on multiple occasions and were absolutely convinced that Ms. Vandermeyden's claims were illegitimate, we had no choice but to end her employment at Tesla."

The one thing Musk and Tesla understood that Kalanick and Uber did not was that Musk and Tesla were one and the same to the public and their stakeholders. Tesla had to respond with the same attention to detail as Musk would. Your personal brand impacts everything you do. The companies you work for, your family, the organizations you join, the schools you attend, and so on. So when Uber sent out a tweet, Kalanick was also accountable. When he yelled on camera to an Uber driver, the company went on public trial along with him.

Kalanick stepped down as CEO at Uber. Tesla became the most valuable car manufacturer in the United States, surpassing Ford and General Motors, even while operating at a loss. CNBC has reported that Tesla burned through $1.2 billion of operating capital in 2017, just as Musk raised another $1.8 billion ($300 million more than expected) in funding.[19]

This outcome shows that investors, stakeholders, executives, and even the average consumer are all starting to see the power of an idea backed by a great story and a strong personal brand. We've examined the differences in the actions of both Musk and Kalanick and discovered that their business choices were not always divergent. It was the way they acted proactively or reactively that had the greatest impact on their individual outcomes.

8 LET'S PLAY A GAME

In business, war, economics, and politics, "game theory" uses mathematical formulas to analyze strategies in competitive situations, where one player's actions depend on those of another. According to Merriam-Webster's dictionary, game theory is "the analysis of a situation involving conflicting interests (as in business or military strategy) in terms of gains and losses among opposing players." Game theory uses mathematical formulas to predict the payoffs and develop strategies accordingly.

It is much easier to explain what situations game theory covers by first explaining what it does not cover. Game theory does not predict outcomes that depend on only one person's actions. For example, let's say Bob told Ann that he would give her fifty dollars to learn the alphabet in Spanish and recite it to him within a week. The only thing standing in Ann's way of getting the fifty dollars from Bob is her own commitment and ability to learn the alphabet in Spanish within the given amount of time. Therefore, the only factor to consider in predicting the possible payoffs is Ann's performance.

Game theory covers situations where there are multiple players and clear payoffs, and each player's payoff depends on the strategies of the others. One of the basic assumptions is that all players in the game are responsible and rational. This is partly why games involving single players are irrelevant: the payoff is simply determined by their actions—can they do it or not?

Game theory is divided into two categories: noncooperative game theory and cooperative game theory.

EXAMPLES OF A NONCOOPERATIVE GAME THEORY SITUATION

A common game that is analyzed in game theory is "the prisoner's dilemma." This involves two players who are both captured, and each of them has to decide whether they are going to give information that will incriminate the other prisoner or keep silent without knowing what the other prisoner will do. If one incriminates the other, that prisoner can go free and the other prisoner goes to jail. If one keeps silent and the other person gives them up, the first one goes to jail and the other prisoner is set free. If they both keep silent, they could get equal or smaller sentences. Or they could each give the other one up, and both would lose. What should they do? Game theory calls this a noncooperative situation, where each of the players is unable to communicate with the other players during the game.

The possible payoffs in the prisoner's dilemma can look like this: If A and B betray each other, each of them serves two years in prison. If A betrays B, but B remains silent, A will be set free and B will serve three years in prison (and vice versa). If A and B both remain silent, each of them will serve only one year in prison (on the lesser charge). In the game, the rational choice for both prisoners would be to turn the other one in. However, in reality, humans tend toward cooperative behavior, which means that they are more likely to try working together than to act in purely rational self-interest.

A REAL-LIFE PRISONER'S DILEMMA

Let's pretend that you rented a house through Airbnb. The host (the person you rented from) neglected to tell you that they live on the property, and it turns out that they will be there during your stay. You want to complain, yet you don't want a negative review on your profile. What are your options? You could complain to Airbnb and receive a discount on your stay, which would leave a negative review on the host's profile, or you could ignore the situation and stay silent. At the same time that you are upset with the host for not disclosing that they would be living on the property with you, the host is upset with you because you did not mention that you smoke. (It bothers them, even though you only smoke outside). They could say something to Airbnb and take money from your security deposit, which would leave you with a negative review, or they could ignore it and say nothing at all. If you both complain to Airbnb, then you both receive a negative review and no additional benefit.

A few of the possible options are reflected in the table opposite. The rational choice would be to complain and try to get a discount. The best outcome (payoff) for both parties would result from choosing to say nothing at all. You might say nothing and leave a negative review anyway, but so could the other person.

In a shared economy, we are often faced with the prisoner's dilemma. Uber allows riders to rate drivers and vice versa, but neither party can see what the other says about them. When we complain to companies that offer a shared service, there is a possibility that while we receive a refund or credit, the other person receives retribution.

Prisoner's Delimma Scenarios

OUTCOME A		OUTCOME B	
Host complains and leaves a negative review; they collect your security deposit.	You say something in person but not online.	Host says something in person but not online.	You complain and leave a negative review; you receive a partial refund on your stay.
Host	Guest	Host	Guest
+1	-2	-2	+1

OUTCOME C		OUTCOME D	
Host says something in person but not online.	You say something in person but not online.	Host complains and leaves a negative review.	You complain and leave a negative review.
Host	Guest	Host	Guest
0	0	-1	-1

The purpose of noncooperative game theory is to predict the other person's strategy in order to win a payoff. In the example above, the payoff would be to gain financial reimbursement with no negative review (Outcome B, Guest), or to reach what is called the Nash equilibrium (named for John Forbes Nash Jr., the subject of the film *A Beautiful Mind*). The Nash equilibrium is the concept that "I have nothing to gain by leaving a negative review, and the other person has nothing to gain by leaving a negative review; therefore, I can assume that neither of us will leave a negative review because that is the best possible outcome." Players are in Nash equilibrium when they each choose the strategy that gives them the best possible payoff, given that the other player is not going to change their strategy. This is the theory that can explain why we have not yet had a nuclear war (because there would be no winner).

The concept behind noncooperative game theory is that it requires competition between individual players. There is nothing within the game itself to enforce cooperation, and no player can affect the outcome by changing their own strategy. This explains why it is in every player's interest to choose the strategy with the best solution. Compromise comes into play when there is something to lose but nothing to gain, which is what allows the compromise to occur.

COOPERATIVE GAME THEORY

In game theory, a cooperative game includes multiple players working together toward the same goal, with the possibility that external factors (such as legal contracts) are forcing the collaboration.

Let's say you have what is called a coalition, or a group of players in a cooperative game. Within each game, every player contributes to the task differently; thus all of the gains or costs for the group should be divided according to the value that each player adds. This is called the Shapley value. This divided approach to groups could be as simple as a group of students working on a project together or as complex as a group of scientists working to solve global warming.

The main goal of the Shapley value is to decide who gets what, what is fair, and how to determine this. For instance, does the CEO add more value than the executive assistant, and how should those differences be awarded? The Shapley value breaks out these ideas into four axioms, or mathematical rules, which are important to understand.

1. Marginal contribution: Each player's value is determined by what is gained or lost by removing them from the game. In other words, if we are working together at a company where our job is to make sales calls, and when you take a day off we make three hundred fewer calls, then your value is three hundred calls, because that is what we lost.

2. Interchangeable players: This rule states that anyone who could be exchanged for another player with no clear loss to the other players is considered interchangeable. Think of two people who have the same role in a company. In theory, they should be paid the same amount of money and be required to contribute the same amount of work.

3. Contribute nothing; receive nothing: This rule is based on what each person puts into the work and how much they should get back. This only matters in situations when someone could potentially contribute but does not. It excludes instances when the group has already decided what they would give to a member who cannot contribute, such as when people go on medical leave at work. Those people cannot contribute but they get paid, which is very different from not contributing when they could have.

4. Cost or payment based on the various parts: The cost and reward should be based on the part of the day that the work actually took place—or should have taken place but did not. For instance, if you worked with someone for six hours on Wednesday, you should both be paid for the six hours. But if you worked three hours on Thursday and your co-worker worked six, then you should be paid for three and he or she should be paid for six.

All of these rules for cooperation can be used to create fair partnerships and teams. They can also help you identify opportunities for developing your personal brand within an organization.

GAME THEORY IN PERSONAL BRAND STRATEGY: MY JOURNEY TO A MILLION-PLUS FOLLOWERS

When I first started to build my following online, I knew that it would take a long time and many hours to develop an audience. My first approach was to look for ways to achieve my goals more quickly and efficiently than others. I decided to use game theory and informational social influence to build my following.

I began by looking at the verified accounts on Twitter. The sign of verification is a blue check mark next to a name, which Twitter gives to an account to verify that people are who they say they are. The original point of Twitter's verification was to help people identify celebrities, news organizations, media, publishers, reporters, and others who can easily be impersonated. Until late 2016, getting verified on Twitter was somewhat of a mystery. Though it started out as a way to identify public figures and media, it came to be a symbol of elite status. When we look at social media from a noncooperative (competitive) game theory perspective, we can see the number of followers and the blue check marks as a way to identify who is important and who is ahead in the game.

From an informational-social-influence perspective, the blue check mark can be seen as an identifier of authority, like social media accounts with many followers. What I needed was to gain more followers with a lot of followers or followers who were verified on Twitter, while working to get myself verified by Twitter, too.

The main thing to consider is that game theory assumes most of us will choose to play by the rules established by Twitter and society, even though these rules are not enforced. With game theory, we assume that most people would allow the check mark for public figures, and they would take the proper steps to become qualified for verification. We assume that the average person will follow the rules for gaining followers. We also assume that those who have many followers do not follow many people and that those without followers only follow people whom they know, have heard of, or want to hear from.

We can also assume that the owners of verified accounts believe that they possess special knowledge about Twitter and identify themselves as authorities. This suggests that they may not play by the same rules as people with accounts that are not verified.

Here's another way to look at it. Twitter is built on the assumption that every person (player in the game) will connect with people they know and follow or connect with others based on their postings and how they perceive the content (or because they are celebrities). Twitter will then suggest other accounts to follow based on the types of accounts people currently follow, communicate with, or have a shared interest in.

The first thing I needed to do was to gain trust, and in order to do so, I needed to identify the following trust signals:

» Reliability (being consistent)

» Effective feedback (responding to people)

» Credibility (having a recommendation, such as a verified account or more than one million followers, including influential followers)

Next, I needed to identify the centers of influence—the most influential accounts on the subjects of digital marketing and social media. If I wanted to be the central thought leader for digital marketing, I would need to be connected (linked) to the most influential accounts.

Finally, I needed a schedule strategy that increased trust signals to my audience—not a schedule for posting but a schedule for communicating. At this point, I had seen many people posting schedule strategies that weren't getting accounts to the level I envisioned for mine, which was to have a hyperengaged and hyperfocused following.

I decided that the best way to create trust signals was to set up a Twitter chat to create a conversation. Twitter chats can be used for many different industries and topics. For example, I have subsequently done this for clients in the health care, insurance, and publishing industries. A Twitter chat tells your followers that you are available to communicate with them once or twice per week (or whatever your schedule allows).

Now I needed to find out, Where is the central group of people who would be interested in my topic? I did some research to learn where the majority of people who care about social media and digital marketing live. I confirmed that London, San Francisco, New York, and Los Angeles were the cities where the interest was concentrated. Then I chose a time to host the Twitter chat that suited all time zones, to ensure that anyone in those areas could attend. I went with 12 noon, Pacific Standard Time (3 p.m. in New York and 8 p.m. in London), and I hosted the chat on a Tuesday.

In order for the Twitter chat to work, I needed a hashtag for people to join. The hashtag would create a separate feed within Twitter, similar to having my own channel. I chose to be referred to as "The Social Media Girl" and used the hashtag #TheSMGirl. (Yes, I realize that the initials could allude to something else, but I think that helped the traffic and added a bit of humor when unsuspecting people attended.)

With the hashtag #TheSMGirl, I scheduled a chat every Tuesday about social media and digital marketing news. I would send out the topic every Monday, and on Tuesday I would prepare five to ten questions around the topic. I used the chat hour to pose these questions to the audience, and they would answer them. During the chats, I would learn things I didn't know and answer whatever I did know.

I sent my Twitter chat to Twitter chat directories (websites that keep calendars of Twitter chats) so that people could easily find and join my chat.

My first Twitter chat looked like this.

> Tweet number one: My #TheSMGirl Twitter chat starts in one hour today, Tues. at 12 p.m. PT! Today's topic is "How to use Facebook groups for community building."

> Tweet number two: My #TheSMGirl Twitter chat is starting now! Today's topic: "How to use Facebook groups for community building."

The chat would appear in the form of the questions below. I would use Q1 for the first question, Q2 for the next one, and so on. People would use A1 for the first answer (and so on) to keep track of their responses. I would always include my hashtag, #TheSMGirl, to keep the chat in a separate feed on Twitter. I would also space the questions out by five to ten minutes, to give people a chance to answer and participate in real time. Here is an example.

Q1: What are some ways that Facebook groups can help drive community? #TheSMGirl

Q2: What are some ways that you can get people to join your Facebook community from other sites? #TheSMGirl

Q3: What are some of your favorite Facebook groups, and what makes them unique? #TheSMGirl

Whenever someone answered a chat question, I would immediately add them to a Twitter list that I created and titled "TheSMGirl chat." If they were already on the Twitter list, I would respond by saying "Welcome back, [Name] #TheSMGirl" so that they would appreciate the response, feel involved, and come back. If they were not on a list, I would add them and then welcome them to the chat.

Many people who responded would not include the hashtag in their response. I would message them and say, "Thank you for joining the chat. Please use the hashtag #TheSMGirl in your responses so that everyone can follow along."

During the Twitter chats, I would solicit engagement from the accounts that I had identified earlier as centers of influence. The idea was that they would have no choice but to respond if several people in the chat were engaged in the pursuit of their response. Once they responded, I would be connected via conversation in Twitter, which would increase my trust signals to their followers and to Twitter.

I have created a digital manual for those of you who want to create your own Twitter chats. You can find it at: cynthialive.com/platform. The Twitter chat digital manual includes a how-to, chat directories, and tools.

What did the Twitter chat do for my brand? Twitter is not just about having followers, it is about having the right kind of followers so that you can influence certain vertical markets, or specific industries—in my case, digital marketing. When I hosted the Twitter chats, people responded repeatedly using digital marketing keywords. Bloggers would write about the chats afterward and hyperlink back to my Twitter profile. This told Twitter and Google that all of these people had come to me for advice on digital marketing.

I would then urge people to subscribe to my Twitter list, "The Social Media Girl." The more people who subscribed, the more trusted the list became. Even if people weren't following me on Twitter, if they had engaged with me and I had added them to the list, they were closely linked to me because the subscribers of the list confirmed its value.

By repeating this process, I became a suggested person to follow on Twitter, by Twitter, for anyone looking for advice on digital marketing. By facilitating the conversation, I became an authority on the topic. For an example of how effective it was to focus my content and host the Twitter chat, take a look at the following influencer studies.

In December 2016, *Inc.* magazine published an article backed by original research and titled "The Influencers That Digital Marketers Are Following on Twitter." I was number twelve, sandwiched between Seth Godin (number eleven) and Guy Kawasaki (number thirteen).

In September 2017, Onalytica released a study showing the most influential people in the following topic areas:

    Social Media

    Sales

    Analytics and Data

    Video

    B2B (business-to-business marketing)

    Writing

Influencer Marketing

Agency (marketing agency)

Lead Generation (finding new business leads via digital marketing and the internet)

Content Strategy (bringing more people to your website by creating better content)

The study identified the top twenty-five influencers in each category. In social media, I was the twenty-second most influential; in video, I was third; in writing, I was twelfth; in influencer marketing, I came in at twentieth; in agency, I came in at eighth; in content strategy, I was twenty-fourth.

In July 2017, research company Tenfold released a study naming the one hundred most influential marketers. I was number eight, following people such as Gary Vaynerchuk (number one) and Tim Ferris (number three) but before Seth Godin (number sixteen).

I am telling you this because I just started my journey to become an influencer in October 2014. Since then, I have managed to become a leading voice in digital marketing, grow my following to more than a million, become an international speaker, and write for various publications. Did I know what I was talking about? Yes. Am I different from anyone else who has a job in a niche market? No, I'm not.

I grew my followers and my notoriety by studying the algorithms, understanding the rules, and at the same time breaking the rules. I used a Twitter chat to focus my message and draw the right kind of audience. I also used the Twitter chat to captivate the audience I was targeting.

I am a growth hacker. Or, more accurately, I have a friend who is a growth hacker and a very good one. We decided on the type of account I wanted and worked strategically to make it happen. This is how we did it.

I told my friend what kind of audience I wanted, and he created lists of these audiences. I would follow these people based on certain keywords. If I engaged with them, I added them to a Twitter list and never unfollowed them. If I never engaged with them, I eventually unfollowed them. Then I used my Twitter chat to create plenty of opportunities to engage with this audience.

WHAT GAME THEORY HAS TO DO WITH THIS

One of the concepts of cooperative game theory is the value of each player. This means the total value created by the player being in the game (in this case, my being in the game) minus the total value created if the player were not in the game. The more accounts I connected to and the more conversations I started, the more valuable my account became to the overall game.

Another concept I applied from game theory is known as signaling theory. Instead of telling people I am valuable or sending a lot of promotional tweets, I signaled that I was valuable by becoming a hub for communication around a specific topic. When I held the chats, the people who cared could come and everyone could network. Every single account that engaged with my Twitter chat increased my credibility and helped convey that I was someone worth following.

When applying this to Twitter or any other social media growth and personal brand awareness, you have to be objective about yourself. Instead of asking, *What will I gain if I have a lot of followers?* ask yourself, *What will others lose if they were to stop following me?*

When I asked this question, I realized early on (as many of you will) that I needed to be able to add strategic value to anyone who followed me. I started the Twitter chat because I knew as soon as I started following people and they could see a community surrounding my Twitter profile, my own value would be equal to or greater than the value that each participating account perceived in the community around me. This is the argument for having a complete strategy around growth hacking that includes community and the value of its individual members, rather than pursuing growth for growth's sake. This is how you become an influencer and build a brand—by knowing that your true value is only as strong as the community you build, the perceived benefit for its members, and the opportunity for them to influence that network.

Designing Accelerated Growth

As I started to grow followers, I was averaging twenty-five hundred to five thousand each month before I received the blue verification check mark from Twitter. That was when my strategy had to change a bit. I had literally followed all the digital marketers, and whoever was going to follow me was probably already doing so. My next goal was to figure out a different strategy for getting more digital marketers, executives, and entrepreneurs to follow me. (I added entrepreneurs and executives to my target demographic because I was trying to bring in work for our digital marketing agency.)

In game theory and economics, there is a field called mechanism design that runs counter to most of the other concepts in game theory (but with the same assumption that all players in the game will act rationally). With mechanism design, the game is reverse-engineered, so you can use this approach to create the game structure itself, instead of playing a game that already has the rules in place.

In my situation, I used mechanism design (with the help of my growth-hacker friend) to choose Twitter accounts that had the followers I wanted, and to look at why they were following that person or account. For example, I wanted more followers who were concerned with data and information because these areas play a big role in digital marketing. So I would find the accounts that had the most followers who were chief information officers. By connecting with these accounts, I gained credibility in the eyes of their followers, which improved the odds that they would follow me back. (I am now the most followed person by chief information officers on Twitter.) We worked in reverse to determine the center of influence for a particular demographic, create a strategy to engage the center of influence, and then use that engagement as a trust signal to their followers. Later I would follow them, with the assumption that they would now be more likely to follow me back.

When we combine this type of reverse engineering with game theory, we end up at the intersection of computer science and game theory known as algorithmic mechanism design. This subfield combines elements of economics, theoretical computer science, and game theory to give us algorithms.

According to Merriam-Webster's dictionary: "Algorithms by definition are a procedure for solving a mathematical problem (as of finding the greatest common divisor) in a finite number of steps that frequently involves repetition of an operation; *broadly*: a step-by-step procedure for solving a problem or accomplishing some end especially by a computer."

How Do Algorithms Work?

Algorithms are designed to operate by a set of simple rules:

» Each step of an algorithm must be clearly defined.

» An algorithm has an end. When it has completed all of the steps it was programmed to complete, the algorithm ends. So essentially algorithms work in a loop.

» Algorithms act on inputs and outputs. Once the rules are set by defining the expected or possible input, their next moves are based on clearly defined responses. (When A happens, B will always respond to it.)

When using reverse engineering to gain more followers on Twitter and other social media websites and search engines, we need to understand their algorithms. We know that every action that occurs on a social network that is not produced by a human is an action produced by an algorithm. This means that the network's responses to human actions are predetermined.

Since algorithms are built on a loop, every unique action from a human will receive the same unique reaction by the algorithm. If we can define the algorithm's outputs (actions taken by Twitter's algorithm) by specific human actions, we can then perform the actions we know will elicit our desired responses to create a strategy that benefits us.

Your Twitter account is only as valuable to potential Twitter followers as they perceive your most valuable Twitter follower. So you can look at your followers (I use SocialRank) and pull out the most valuable ones by category. Then you can narrow *their* followers down to a category—let's say digital marketing—and you can assume that a large percentage of your most valuable followers' followers will follow you back if you follow them. Why? They assume that you must be worth following if an account they value is following you.

For example, if Barack Obama's Twitter account followed your Twitter account, you could assume that 50 percent or more of his active Twitter followers would follow you just because he follows you.

If your Twitter account follows another Twitter account that is unaware of you, then you are increasing the chances of their seeing your account. Many people refuse to follow other accounts on Twitter because they want their follower ratios (the number of followers you have versus the number of people you are following) to make them look famous. This is why many people prefer to have a much higher percentage of followers than accounts they are following.

Most of us are not famous. Well, maybe *you* are, but the rest of us have to stop treating Twitter and other social media sites the same way that famous people often do and start playing by our own rules to achieve our goals. Stop trying to be famous and start trying to connect with people. Following an account is the easiest way to get in front of your target audience.

Six degrees of separation is actually only 4.67 degrees on Twitter. You've probably heard the expression six degrees of separation, or "six degrees of Kevin Bacon," as it's often referred to in the cultural zeitgeist. This is the idea that everyone is at most six people away from connection to anyone else on the planet. This theory suggests that if I gave you a letter to give to someone you didn't know in another country, it would take a chain of only six people to deliver the letter to that person.

On Twitter, this number is less than six. In 2010, social media data company Sysomos conducted a study to find out how many degrees of separation every Twitter user was from all other users. The company studied 5.2 billion Twitter friendships (someone is following your account and you are following their account back). The results? Everyone on Twitter is only about 5 degrees of separation away from each other. If you are on Twitter and Bob Saget is on Twitter, then you are just about five friendships away from being Twitter friends with Bob Saget. This is known as your friendship distance. In theory, we can connect with anyone on Twitter by combining strategies.

In their study, Sysomos tested the reach of every Twitter account's network. They found that if you visit the profile of every Twitter friend of five people, on average you will encounter 83 percent of all Twitter users. If you visit the profiles of all of the friends of friends of six people, the average jumps to encountering 96 percent of all Twitter users.

What this means is that you don't have to put in too much effort to reach a massive amount of Twitter users. This study was done in 2010, and of course the algorithm, number of Twitter followers, and statistics have changed by now. But for better or worse, they haven't changed drastically, so the message still stands: follow the network and reach a lot of people. On Facebook, there are even fewer degrees of separation.

Having the blue verification check mark on Twitter matters. When you are growing your Twitter followers by growth hacking, it is important to understand that people will follow back verified accounts more often than they will follow back accounts that are not verified. And verified accounts will follow other verified accounts.

Also note, in following and unfollowing accounts, that the number of accounts you can follow is important. If you are not verified, you can follow a thousand accounts per day. When you are verified, that number is closer to twenty thousand accounts per day, or twenty times your follow limit—a huge increase in people following back.

These days, you can submit your Twitter account to become verified. Twitter allows and encourages people and brands to submit for verification. By going to verification.twitter.com/welcome. Back in the day (2013 to 2016), you had only two options. Option one was to have a registered Twitter advertising account and use the link verification.twitter.com. (Technically, we've always had the ability to apply for verification; we just didn't know it.) But this approach was difficult because there were only a couple of reliable ways to get verified: either to have an email address at a major news company or publication, or to have published music on iTunes. Those guys always got verified.

Option two was the approach I used. When I first submitted to be verified, I was denied. This actually dinged me, making it more difficult to get verified. So I convinced someone at the Twitter office to verify me on Christmas Day. (Yes, the day when no one is paying attention because they are with family and friends.) It was the best Christmas gift ever.

Once my growth-hacker friend and I knew some of the algorithmic intentions and human elements of the game, we created a plan. Our plan was built on conversation (Twitter chat), follower lists, the blue verification check mark, and our goals. Now we were ready to reverse engineer my Twitter profile. (If you're interested in growth hacking on social media, I recommend checking out Fanbase to help build your following. They're the best.)

Some of what my friend and I came up with was incredible. We followed the active Twitter followers of my most valuable followers. We went with active members because we knew that they were, well, *active* on Twitter. We targeted people who we thought were likely to retweet based on how many retweets they had given similar topics. We followed and engaged with brands and celebrity profiles that had high follow-back ratios so that we could then target *their* fans. It was amazing.

The rule for gaining more than a million followers (now going on two million) is similar to what I imagine is the rule for becoming ultrawealthy: you have to know the rules so well that you can break them—not just for gain but in order to start to be rewarded by the system in place. When we growth hacked Twitter, we knew the rules so well that we understood after a certain point the algorithm and its loop would eventually start to reward us by suggesting us in feeds, suggesting whom to follow, and increasing views of our tweets.

My accountant told me a memorable story that applies to understanding how to build your brand and grow your audience: "When I drive to work every day, there is a bridge with a toll on my way. If I drive over the bridge and choose not to pay the toll, that is tax evasion. If I choose to find a new route to work, that is tax avoidance, which is completely legal."

The rules set by Twitter are not in the user's favor. They want you to pay the toll to get to a million followers. However, if you find a new way to get there, then you are still playing the game they created and you will be rewarded.

CASE STUDY: HOW I GOT THE LOS ANGELES DODGERS TO FOLLOW ME ON TWITTER

In the summer of 2014, I went to a baseball game at Dodger Stadium with my fiancé and friends. The game was the Los Angeles Dodgers playing the Philadelphia Phillies. My fiancé, as well as my best friend and many of our friends are Phillies fans; I was the only Dodgers fan in the group.

In an effort to throw effective jabs at their team, I looked up interesting facts about the Phillies. What I found was an amazing tweetstorm. As I was tweeting with fans and nonfans, my younger brother saw my tweets and texted me about them. At the time, he was a sophomore at the University of Reno, Nevada, which does not have a baseball team (nor does Las Vegas, where we grew up). Although most of our family was born in the Los Angeles area and we still have family here, my brother had decided not to become a fan of Los Angeles sports teams.

Below is my first tweet from the game that my brother saw, followed by the response from the Dodgers:

After that tweet went out, my brother texted me and started talking trash about the Dodgers. As a fan, I could not let this continue. I immediately saw the opportunity to turn this into a game. I decided to leverage my brother to get the Dodgers to follow me on Twitter, and I sent the team the following tweet:

Dear @Dodgers I will unfollow my brother/ this dodger hater @jpeazy10 if you follow me. Thx ;)

9:10 PM - 23 Apr 2014 from Los Angeles, CA

1 Retweet 5 Likes

My brother (@jpeazy10) immediately returned to texting me. I was his most valuable follower in those days, and he needed me to follow him so that he could gain more influential followers. By that time, I had about twenty-five thousand followers.

When my brother begged me not to unfollow him, I saw it as another play in the game. I took a screenshot of the texts that showed him begging me not to unfollow him, and I went back on Twitter to send the following tweet:

Oh @Dodgers he is begging me not to unfollow him- but I leave it in your hands. You follow me and I'll ditch him

> What will happen? No one knows

Delivered

Please don't you're my most credible follower...

Lol that's hilarious

As you can see from the tweet, things were really heating up. I didn't know whether the Dodgers would follow me, and neither did my brother. Minutes later, the Dodgers followed me on Twitter. Victory was mine, and my brother lost his most credible follower. I wrote a celebratory tweet and then unfollowed my brother.

Cynthia Johnson ✔
@CynthiaLIVE

Shoutout to my new follower @Dodgers - and an apology to my brother @jpeazy10 for choosing the Dodgers over him. #ilovela

9:36 PM - 23 Apr 2014 from Los Angeles, CA

3 Retweets **10** Likes

💬 1   ↻ 3   ♡ 10   ᵢⅼᵢ

9 A THREE-WAY WITH A ROBOT

Networking is everything when it comes to personal branding. Whom you know and how they feel about you is not only important, it is the most valuable part of your brand. Your network is only as vast as you make it and only as valuable as the time you make for it. Everything you want to achieve is in the hands of someone else, and your goals can be informed, accelerated, and guided by your social media networking.

Before we get to the actionables, it is important to understand the type of thinking that allows us to use the available online tools for effective networking. The specific action items change as the algorithms and social media companies change, but the thinking behind them is still relevant. Remember to think outside the box and look for what no one else sees. This is where the real leverage and big wins will always be found.

NETWORKING AND SOCIAL MEDIA

A common misconception about social media is that the conversations you have with other people or brands is between you and them. The truth is that any conversation you have online is a three-way conversation among you, the person you are communicating with, and a machine. In the world of game theory, anyone who can impact your personal outcome is in the game and must be accounted for. If you send an email that goes into a spam folder, this will impact your relationship with the person you assume received your email but never responded. If you tag someone on Facebook and that person never sees the message because they were bombarded that day with tons of messages or alerts and missed your message, it will impact your relationship with them. You can also flip the situation to imagine that you missed a message in your feed, and that changed the way someone thought of you. It was out of your control: you didn't mean to miss the message, you will never know either way, yet your communication with that person may be tarnished forever.

When you are networking online, by phone, or in any other situation that requires a machine or person to move your message along, you must also factor in how the presence of that third party may impact your relationship. That machine or person can be the determining factor in the success of your relationship.

Networking is about communicating the right message, the right recommendation, the right place, and the right time, combined with how we can help each other. It is no secret that the world has become more connected, and the people in it have become busier than ever as a result. The busier we get, the more we need to justify how our time is spent. Some of you have never lived in a less-busy world, and others will remember a time when you wouldn't contact anyone outside of your preplanned day until you got home. The perfect understanding of networking in the modern world is a combination of these perspectives.

However, there are positives to being in a three-way relationship when you are networking. The machines (algorithms) can be very useful for climbing the networking ladder. They tell us things about people that we would not have known without their involvement. They connect us by interest, and they connect us by mutual friends or acquaintances. If you think of the social media platforms as a third person in a conversation, you can network more effectively.

To do this, you have to consider what everyone in the situation has to gain or lose, including the social media and communication platform itself. Let's start with the robot, the machine, the algorithm—the social media tool that stands between you and the person you want to connect with. What do social media sites have to gain? In order to use these tools as effectively as possible, it is important to understand what they need from your relationship.

HOW TO GAUGE THE NEEDS OF THE ALGORITHM

If you want to understand the needs of the social media websites and their algorithms, you have to start by following the money. In other words, follow the news around corporate partnerships, new product launches, and investments. This information makes it extremely easy to figure out what is of value for the company at a given time.

First of all, money is the most important thing for these companies. They spend their time trying to find new ways to make money. Second, social media companies want users, and they want these users to feel safe. Third, they want to prevent spam of any kind. Last, they want to outdo the competition and take away their competitors' audiences.

How does this apply to networking? There are many ways to connect with people online. Look at the most popular social media platforms and search engines used for communication today, and you can see how many ways each one provides for connecting with other people. Let's review the various ways to connect with someone on these social media platforms so that you can utilize them in your networking strategy. To start, take a look at some of the ways you can communicate with another person on Facebook, LinkedIn, Twitter, and Instagram.

Facebook

- » Sending a friend request
- » Unfriending a person
- » Muting someone's profile
- » Following someone
- » Commenting on a post
- » Sharing a post
- » Posting on someone's Facebook page
- » Liking a post
- » Tagging someone in a post or image
- » Inviting people to an event
- » Inviting people to a group
- » Creating a group messenger
- » Sending a private message
- » Calling someone on Facebook Messenger
- » Poking someone
- » Suggesting a friend to someone
- » Fund-raising
- » Checking in to a location
- » Inviting someone to a game you are playing
- » Buying or selling something

LinkedIn

- » Connecting with a person
- » Following an account
- » Following a company
- » Tagging a person in a post
- » Tagging a company in a post
- » Adding and tagging a company or organization on your profile
- » Joining a group
- » Posting to a group
- » Creating a group
- » Inviting someone to a group
- » Sending a private message
- » Applying for a job
- » Posting a job
- » Accessing someone's email
- » Viewing someone's profile so they can see you viewed it
- » Blogging
- » Using the Profinder search to find freelancers
- » Sharing the content of an individual or company
- » Creating a SlideShare
- » Following someone on SlideShare

Twitter

- » Favoriting a tweet
- » Retweeting a tweet
- » Posting a tweet
- » Commenting on a tweet
- » Following a Twitter account
- » Unfollowing a Twitter account
- » Blocking a Twitter account
- » Adding someone to a Twitter list
- » Following a list that someone else created
- » Mentioning a Twitter account in a tweet
- » Tagging people in a tweet
- » Sending a private message
- » Adding a tweet to a moment
- » Reporting a tweet to Twitter
- » Reporting an account to Twitter
- » Linking to a tweet
- » Linking to a Twitter profile
- » Embedding a tweet
- » Muting a Twitter account

Instagram

- » Following an account
- » Unfollowing an account
- » Blocking an account

- » Tagging a profile in a post

- » Mentioning a profile in a post

- » Commenting on a post

- » Mentioning someone in the comment on a post

- » Sharing an Instagram post privately to another account

- » Sharing a post to Instagram

- » Creating an Instagram collection

- » Creating an Instagram story

As you can see from the many ways of connecting on social media platforms, creating a networking strategy is a must. The best place to start is to determine what you need from the desired relationship. Are you looking for a job? A recommendation? A mentor or someone who can help you with your new venture? Whatever you need, make sure your objectives are clear. Once you have done that, you're ready to devise your strategy.

There are steps to keep in mind when you are devising a networking plan. Ideally, you want to make sure the other person sees you before you reach out to them. This is a longer networking play. Spend a few days making them aware that you exist, that you are interested in connecting with them, and that you will eventually reach out. This step requires breaking out your communication according to day and account type. You can also use the lists of ways to communicate on each of the social media platforms to write your own playbook. Use what you know about each platform, and identify which platforms the person you want to network with is using. Here, I have outlined an example of how a long-term play can work.

Day One: Look at the person's LinkedIn profile. Make sure that your privacy settings allow people to see that you looked at their profiles. (This only works if they actually see you viewing their profile.) Before taking the next step, check to see whether the person has reciprocated and looked at your account. If they have, add them on LinkedIn as a connection, with a message like this: "I found your account while looking for [insert whatever you were looking for] and noticed that we also have [insert something from their profile] in common. It's great to meet like-minded people in the area of [insert whatever your common ground is]."

Day Two: If they haven't looked at your profile, find them on Twitter and follow them there.

Day Three: Retweet something they have posted on Twitter, and then add them to a Twitter list.

Day Four: Add them on LinkedIn, with a note that says something like this: "I found you on LinkedIn while looking for [insert what you were looking for], and your background is incredible. I also saw on Twitter that we have [insert whatever you have in common or a mutual connection] in common. LinkedIn is a great place to connect, but if you have the time, I would also like to connect by phone or email about [insert what you are asking of them]. If you're like me, you probably have a busy schedule and your time is limited. I figure if we start now we can get something on the calendar in the coming weeks."

Day Five: If they still have not accepted your connection, you want to connect with three people who are in their network, closely associated with them, and active in LinkedIn groups. (People who have time to post in LinkedIn groups have time to connect and are looking for more connections.)

The goal for Day One is to find a way for them to know that you viewed their account. This is the first step in putting yourself in front of the person. Look through the list of possible ways to communicate with people on social media to see if there are any other options that can help you achieve this goal. Day Two's goal is to let the person know you are viewing them on a different profile, so they can see that you were looking specifically for them and that it was not mere chance or the algorithms that brought you together. Day Three's goal is to show the person that not only are you looking at their profiles and searching specifically for them but you are also engaged in their content. Day Four's goal is to make your first attempt to connect (if the person hasn't reached out to you yet). Day Five's goal is to revisit the strategy if you haven't yet connected. If you have already connected, the goal is always to take the conversation to a face-to-face coffee meeting or phone call. You want to remove the third-party (algorithm, machine, or robot) from your relationship. One-on-one communication is not only more effective but it is also more meaningful. Not many people want to share their personal relationships. Since we consider social media tools and algorithms as players in this game, we understand that they are the third "person" that needs to be removed for a short time so that a meaningful relationship can blossom.

In most cases, people are not ignoring you when you reach out; the real issue is inbox fatigue. It takes me days to see a LinkedIn message because I get so many of them. I never see Twitter messages because my Twitter inbox is full of spam. If I get a cold call, I won't answer it. If you send me a cold email, it will take me more than a week to get to it, and I will be reading it after my work hours, so my focus won't be entirely sharp. But if you send me an Instagram message, I will see it right away and get back to you. Why? You have to target people where they are not overwhelmed with messages or requests. The preceeding plan is just one example of how to connect with someone online. What you should be thinking about are your goals for each step of this process, not the steps themselves.

Once you schedule that coffee or phone meeting, you want to prepare a meeting strategy. One of your goals should always be to figure out how you can be of help to the other person. Sometimes this can be very straightforward: some people may simply tell you what they need. Other times it will be a bit more difficult, and you'll have to figure it out. In this situation, think of your network. Whom do you know that this person would want to know, and vice versa? If you don't have the ability to help a person directly, you may be able to help them indirectly by introducing them to someone you know. After all, we are less than five degrees away from everyone else, so an introductory chain could lead anywhere.

The other thing you want to get from your meeting is a clear next step, even if that is to never speak again (but hopefully it won't be). Your next step could be to send an introduction between them and someone else, or to follow through on an action. I like to follow up with an email after my calls, to provide links to things I mentioned in the call or just to recap our conversation and let people know they can reach out again.

NETWORKING ADVICE FOR YOUR PROFILES

Consider these four things to enhance your social media profiles and optimize them for networking.

Always Include Your Email and What You Can Be Reached For

Put your email in your social media profiles, along with a note that lets people know you want them to connect with you and what you wish to connect over. You can follow and connect with people all day long, but unless they know how and why to reach out to you, the ball will remain in your court. It is also important that you make the right kinds of information available.

There are a few ways to do this. I have a separate email account for my social media profiles, which is connected to my blog and personal website. I keep it separate from my personal and work email accounts. I check my social media emails once a week, allowing myself time to respond to them. When I want people to email me, I use the message "I've got five minutes; let's connect!" on all of my social media profiles. You can either use mine (I borrowed it from someone else) or create your own. Don't skip adding it, though. The opportunities that will come your way if you create a path for them can be astonishing. Take the time to set up a communication flow that works for you.

Don't Post All the Time

This may seem counterintuitive when it comes to personal branding and social media. The assumption is that the more content you post, the more people will see it, and the more notice you will get. While this may be true, quality is what really matters, not quantity. For most people who are using personal branding for their businesses and careers, the more they post, the worse the content. When executives and professionals who are not internet celebrities post all day long, it decreases their audiences' perception of their power. People begin to question how they could be excellent at their jobs when they spend so much of their time uploading links that few people will actually read.

Instead, here are the acceptable reasons to post: to share content you have written, to respond to content about you, to share an opinion, to communicate something or ask a question, to celebrate and congratulate others. These are all appropriate social media actions for professionals. Do not post multiple times a day, because when someone lands on your profile (if you use a growth hacker, this happens often), they will see a lot of garbage content that has pushed down the relevant content. Don't clutter your feed with content that doesn't genuinely add something of value.

Avoid Overusing Hashtags

When hashtags are misused or overused, they can become the digital version of "Look at me! Look at me! I am trying to grow my followers!" You don't want that. Hashtags were originally intended for creating chat groups, following events or sports games, or starting a movement on Twitter. They were great when Twitter's search algorithm was young and still learning. The hashtags helped feed the algorithm information, which helped with targeting in advertising (hence the need for the robot). It was never meant for tagging random words in your posts. The main purpose of the hashtag on all social media channels is to create live public groups around topics or interests.

Yet we see professionals posting on social media with multiple hashtags. For example, "Just spoke at #RandomConference so #blessed to be here as a #speaker talking about #leadership and #Sales! #hustle #travel," sends the message that they are building their brands. Announcing that you are branding is the opposite of being helpful with your branding, and it shows that you are just now learning social media. If this is you, don't worry; it happens to the best of us. Just stop doing it and think before you #. You want to use hashtags to start a group, to follow an event, or to be funny, like #hashtag or #IAmSoBasic. I've created a manual to show you how, which you can find at cynthialive.com/platform.

The most important people don't have a lot of followers on social media. This fact has been a game changer in my networking strategy. The most accomplished people to know do not have a huge Twitter following, but many of them are on Twitter. You can easily do a Twitter search for "executives at NASA" or "female executives at Facebook" or "editor" (my favorite). These people are extremely busy, and while they want to understand Twitter or other social media platforms, they don't have the time to learn how to use them as effectively as they could. This is where the robot in the relationship can be helpful. Once you find these people on Twitter, instead of emailing them like everyone else does, send them a Twitter message. They will respond. If you get a lot of Twitter messages and are afraid of missing the response, you can check back or leave your email address in the message and ask them to email you.

When I attended the World Government Summit in Dubai, I heard Helen Clark, former prime minister of New Zealand and then administrator of the United Nations Development Program (UNDP), speak. I was attending the pre-event event as media and was not granted a face-to-face interview with her. So I went to her Twitter feed and saw her Snapchat handle in her Twitter bio, which said "Follow me on Snapchat." I immediately added her on Snapchat and sent her a video message of me live from the event, saying, "I heard that you left early, but I really wanted to connect. If there is another option to meet, please let me know!"

Within minutes, Helen Clark responded to my snap (mind you, this is a United Nations leader and former world leader) and said, "Please email this person, and we can start the conversation." The email she gave me was for one of her assistants at the United Nations, and—boom!—just like that, I was in touch with Helen Clark. This worked because she had told me (and everyone else) on Twitter how and where to communicate with her. She was also just learning how to use Snapchat, so she was responding to messages there more than anywhere else. On Snapchat there was no competition for her time. In fact, I'll bet she was even excited that someone sent her a message there. I was not only letting her know that I wanted to interview her but also confirming that her Snapchat messaging was getting through to people.

The takeaway here is to find people in the places where you have the most leverage and the least competition for their time and attention—regardless of whether they are world leaders, executives, or celebrities. In a three-way, there is always one person who feels neglected or like the weakest link in the relationship. This can cause the person who feels neglected to overcompensate by doing too much, working too hard for the relationship, and that will ultimately cause the relationship dynamic to shift.

Treat Everyone as if They Matter, Because They Do

Don't be the person who ignores the little guy, because in a connected digital world, you never know how people will grow from one day to the next. I have been snubbed many times by "experts" at conferences, events, and online, who now love to tell people that they work with me. I also remember people who attended my Twitter chats and wanted to learn from me, who have now far surpassed me in the same industry. Even if the message is that you are busy, try your best to respond to their questions. I hate nothing more than to see a person shamed by an "expert" for asking a question at a conference, when the entire point of attending is for them to learn. Being a figurehead comes with responsibility.

Still, to truly embrace the idea of treating everyone equally, most people need to know what's in it for them. Around 2009 or 2010, I went to an event called Blog World. I happened to meet someone at the event, we connected on LinkedIn, but I later forgot about him. Then one day when I was on LinkedIn, I realized that my network had suddenly opened up a lot. I was receiving many requests from people I didn't know, who had all started following a specific person. When I looked him up, I recognized the face but not the name, and I saw that he had recently updated his job title to CEO at Buzzfeed. Just like that, my network went wild. Someone I had randomly met at a conference years earlier just got a promotion and was sharing the benefit indirectly with his network. From that moment on, all of his connections became second connections to me on LinkedIn, which meant that it was one hundred times easier for me to grab the attention of all his friends. (When you are the CEO at Buzzfeed, you make a lot of friends.) So go ahead and connect with people; it doesn't hurt, and you never know how much it could eventually help.

INTERNET LAWS TO HELP YOU UNDERSTAND HOW TO COMMUNICATE ONLINE

The 1 Percent Rule: Only 1 percent of the people online create content; the other 99 percent are lurkers. As an example from Wikipedia, 90 percent of the participants of a community only view content, 9 percent of the participants edit content, and 1 percent of the participants actively create new content. This means that if you don't participate, you are essentially facilitating a monopoly on information control and digestion.

Wiio's Laws

Communication usually fails—except when it unexpectedly succeeds. To put it more specifically:

If communication can fail, it will.

If communication cannot fail, it will probably still fail.

If your communication style seems to be succeeding as you intended, there is some sort of misunderstanding.

If you become content with your communication style, it will fail you.

If your message leaves anything open to interpretation, it will be interpreted in the most negative way possible.

When dealing with mass communication, what things appear to be is more important than what they are.

Overcommunication, clear communication, and requesting confirmation of communication are a must. When dealing with anyone who reaches out to you, or when reaching out to them, make sure there is no room for interpretation. Anything you say that can be read, can be interpreted incorrectly. (Remember Poe's Law, page 94?)

The Streisand Effect

If you try to hide, remove, or censor a piece of information on the internet, that piece of information becomes more interesting. It will likely have the unintended consequence of ending up in a public forum or media outlet. This law was created after Barbra Streisand tried to keep images of her home off the internet, and the internet responded by adding her public information to file-sharing websites. If you are trying to keep something off the internet and out of the media, don't be obvious about it. The more they find what you don't want to be found, the more value people attach to finding and exposing it.

Segal's Law

A man with a watch knows what time it is. A man with two watches is never sure. If you are going to state an opinion publicly, make sure that you have only one opinion on the topic. If you have two opinions or are unsure, avoid the topic publicly until you *are* sure.

Cunningham's Law

The best way to get the right answer on the internet is not to ask a question; it's to post the wrong answer. "The pen is mightier than the sword": you can accomplish a lot with your words, so choose them wisely. "Many a true word is spoken in jest": according to Poe's Law, many words written in jest will be perceived as true.

Skitt's Law

Any post correcting an error in another post will contain at least one error. The likelihood of an error in a post is directly proportional to the embarrassment it will cause the poster. Don't take yourself too seriously; everyone makes mistakes. The more you let them affect you, the more you will make.

The Law of Exclamation

The more exclamation points used in an email or post, the more likely it is that the message is untrue. The same holds true for the excessive use of capital letters. If you write in a passive-aggressive manner, your audience may come to dislike you.

Umhoefer's Rule

Articles on writing are all too frequently poorly written.

CASE IN POINT: FIND A MENTOR ON LINKEDIN

When I first took on a leadership role at a company, I began to question whether I actually had as much empathy as I had always thought. Being a manager and a boss required a skill set that was outside of mine. I was great at delegating tasks, getting things done, and organizing a team, but handling the personal aspects of the job was not one of my strengths.

When employees came to me with personal issues, I wouldn't know what to say or how to help. I had little patience for deliverables not getting done on time or projects going in unintended directions. I also struggled with leading effective meetings, because information was getting lost in the translation. My reports would just nod silently in agreement with me, even if I was wrong. These issues needed to be fixed, and I knew that the fix had to begin with me.

I decided that I would find a mentor. My criteria were that the person be local, have available time for me, and be an expert in communication, leadership, and team building. I needed someone outside of my work situation, who didn't know me and could look objectively at the obstacles I was facing.

I went on LinkedIn and started to do searches for people who fit this criteria. It was easy to find locals, experts, and people outside my network, but it was fairly difficult to determine whether someone had enough time to spend with me. I wanted a career person who had lived through a similar situation, but many of these people were busy doing their own work. At that time, I was subscribed to the *Harvard Business Review*, so I went on LinkedIn and joined the Harvard Business Review group to begin my search for a mentor. That's when I found Dr. Mark Goulston.

Mark Goulston is the ideal leadership coach. He is patient, accomplished, caring, and passionate about his work. He has written several books, including *Just Listen*, which were even suggested to me by people who were unaware of our relationship. Mark is the lead mentor at the China Foundation, and he works with the Los Angeles

Police Department to train students on how to behave when they get pulled over (what they call the POP Protocol). He also writes for the *Harvard Business Review*, has lectured at UCLA and USC, and is a neuroscientist and psychologist. These days, he is also a consultant, speaker, trainer, and coach for organizations such as IBM, Goldman Sachs, and Merrill Lynch.

If you think he sounds like the ideal mentor and that he must be insanely busy, you're right. But what struck me about Mark was his behavior in the Harvard Business Review group on LinkedIn. The group had more than one million members, and they were not allowed to accept more members at the time. (LinkedIn now allows more than one million members per group.) Out of all the members in the group, Mark was the most active. He posted frequently, he always responded, and he put remarkable time and effort into his responses.

When I saw all this, I realized that Mark either cared enormously about his work or had a lot of time on his hands—or both. He seemed like just the person I was looking for. So I sent him a request to connect on LinkedIn, but I neglected to leave a message. I was extremely nervous about connecting with him, because he is a really well-known expert in his field. Reaching out to a person with his background, credentials, and experience can trigger fear of rejection but I pushed through it and messaged him anyway.

To my great surprise, Mark accepted my request with the following message:

10/16/2014

Interesting and impressive background you have. What is your current focus and what do you want to do and be when you grow up?

All the best,

Mark

1:22 PM

I can assure you that in 2014 my background showed nothing particularly interesting or impressive. I spent the next two hours crafting a response, but all I could come up with was:

10/16/2014

Hello!

I do believe that you are the impressive one here!

My current focus is building a team and a business. I am a big believer in the power of teamwork.

I want to be a student when I grow up. I certainly hope that my mind is the last thing to go.

Honestly, it is great to connect with you. What are you currently doing (other than writing best selling books)? Is there anything I can do to help?

Thank you!

Cynthia

3:29 PM

As you can see from my email, I was hinting that I needed help with managing a team. The business I reference here is my online social media and thought-leader brand. I was not a business owner, but I did have a team. Today I cringe at my use of exclamation points in this message. You know—that feeling you get when you talk about the old version of yourself that no longer reflects who you are?

Despite my exclamation overuse, Mark responded:

"Hello back at you. I'm doing lots. Writing my next book, creating a course with the American Management Association around my book *Just Listen* (which became the top book on listening in the world), working with a company in China to help American expat managers at Fortune 500 companies to better cooperate with Chinese workers outside the big cities in China.

Something you might find interesting is this presentation which is wowing CEO audiences: What Steve Jobs Knew—How to Create Insanely Excited Customers at: http://markgoulston.com/beingstevejobs. I have figured out how to teach people to look at the world through Steve Jobs' eyes, and it is getting amazing ratings. Say more about your building a team and a business."

He had responded in minutes, requesting more information, and I was back at square one. So what did I do? Like a dummy, I tried to speak to him as though I were at his level, took hours to craft a response, and then—like the newbie that I was—sent him a response at 12:59 a.m. No one sends emails at 12:59 a.m. after sending a message with so many exclamations. All I could think was, He probably thinks I am neurotic, and maybe I am neurotic? But my response was:

"I would love to know more about your company in China. I studied Mandarin for a couple of years and have traveled throughout China. I have many ex-pat friends that work for Chinese companies. After speaking with them throughout the years, the thing that I always found to be a huge barrier in the communication between ex-pats and Chinese workers is the initial hiring of an ex-pat. The Chinese companies often pay them more (I speak for Chinese companies, not American companies in China) and at that same time treat them as a higher-valued asset even if they're not. I think from an ex-pat's perspective, this is great in the beginning, but after some time the desire to actually be held responsible for something becomes frustrating.

"My business is digital marketing and leadership. I am the Director of Social Media Marketing at RankLab, a digital marketing agency in Santa Monica, CA. I am also the new editorial director and global board member for Social Media Club, and I speak at marketing conferences sometimes.

"I am currently building two teams, and it is much easier said than done. I have my team at the agency and the international editorial team for Social Media Club, which is global and remote.

"Finding yourself in a leadership position is the strangest thing in the world. The great conundrum. I will definitely take a look at your work on the Steve Jobs method. Sounds like it will be more than worth the read."

In responding to Mark, I tried to sound cool by discussing what I knew about expats in China, which wasn't a lot. When I said, "I speak at marketing conferences sometimes," at that time I had spoken at one—literally the week prior to sending this email. I referred to my leadership problems but never actually addressed them or asked for help. And what is the great conundrum? Then I referenced his work with the Steve Jobs method and said I would read it. He sent me the link to a video.

In reality, this email exchange should have been a failure and a learning experience, but instead, it became an opportunity and a learning experience. It turned out that Mark was also a night owl. He messaged me again at 1:19 a.m. saying:

10/17/2014

 Hi Cynthia,

I am also in Santa Monica. Seems like we should meet.

Best,

Mark

1:19 AM

What? He was willing to meet me, and I didn't even have to ask? I was so shocked that I responded with more exclamation marks, of course.

I met Mark for coffee in Santa Monica the following week. He brought me a copy of his book, and he asked a lot of questions about what I was dealing with, my goals, and so on. After hearing my responses, he said, "I think I should mentor you." I was trying to play it cool, but after the meeting I freaked out. Later I introduced Mark to some of my digital marketing friends who could help him promote his new book, and he introduced me to, well, literally everyone.

I now meet with Mark every couple of months over dinner, and he helps guide me through my latest work and life issues. He shows up to all of my events and is my biggest cheerleader without letting me get away with anything. When I was applying to schools to get an MBA, Mark wrote me a letter of recommendation. He noted that I was still working on my emotional intelligence, but that he detected no personality issues (and as the expert, he would know).

Years later, Mark is still my ideal mentor. To give you an idea of how much work we have done to help each other (though we only meet a few times a year), take a look at our mutual connections on LinkedIn. When I first met Mark, we had zero mutual connections; we now have 158 and counting. But we still have only one mutual group on LinkedIn: the Harvard Business Review.

Be clear about what you want and what you need. Get creative with your solution, and don't be afraid of failure. If Mark had not responded to my email, we would have forgotten each other, and that would have been the end of the story. Instead, I now have a mentor, friend, and advocate who supports me both in my career and in my life.

10 EVERYONE IS KNOWN FOR SOMETHING

In October 2014, I spoke at a conference for the first time. I had already worked on a case study about how to rank Pinterest boards in Google's search for high-value keywords, and I used this experience to apply for the conference. I was assigned the topic of Pinterest and SEO and asked to create a fifteen-minute presentation. I would be on a panel with two other speakers, who would present on the same topic. In the past, this conference had focused exclusively on SEO, and it had recently added social media tracks. I was a social media person who had recently started to learn about SEO. But in the eyes of traditional attendees, I was nothing. In fact, when I had attended the confence the year before, another participant spotted my name badge and said, "Oh, social media. I don't need to talk to you," and walked away.

Although I was very nervous, I knew that I needed to speak at this conference because my contribution was on a par with what everyone else was sharing. I had never been nervous to speak in front of anyone before. I had been an actor my entire life, I'd been on the debate team, and I'd even sung solo (even though I never really could sing). But this conference was different. I pictured myself standing in front of a room full of people who were in the same field as I was. They could disagree with my theory or believe that the field of social media was meaningless compared to SEO.

A few weeks before the conference, I was put in touch with my two co-speakers: one man who had written a book on the topic of SEO, and another who ran a popular industry publication dedicated to the topic.

The night before I was scheduled to speak, I met someone who would also be speaking at the conference. He asked me about my topic and how long I had been around. After answering, I told him that I was excited but nervous. "What do you have to be nervous about?" he said. "You just have to stand there and look pretty—we men have to have actual good content." Perhaps he was trying to be friendly and calm my nerves, but it had the opposite effect.

I immediately went from feeling nervous to being head-on mission driven. I could not allow anyone to infer that I was there for any reason other than what I had to contribute. I had to take action. What I did next changed my life by forever changing the way I viewed success, opportunity, and position.

I left the event, got on social media, and ran searches for anyone who worked at SlideShare. (The conference expectation was that after your session and your presentation you were to upload your deck of slides to SlideShare and tag the conference.) My plan was to convince SlideShare to feature my deck on their website. This strategy might increase my views and downloads, proving that my content was good enough to be presented to a larger audience who would help decide.

After messaging a few people at SlideShare, I went to bed in preparation for my 9 a.m. presentation. The next day, I woke up late and had to run out of the hotel to grab a taxi. "To the convention center, please," I said as I jumped into the taxi and started applying my mascara. Anyone who has ever been to a conference in Las Vegas should know that there are two convention centers on opposite ends of the strip. Having grown up in Las Vegas, I should have taken this into consideration as the taxi headed to the wrong one.

Some time later, we finally arrived at the correct location with only minutes to spare. I rolled into the conference hall, frazzled, to see my co-workers and about a hundred people seated as the moderator was opening. I hustled to the stage and accepted my default position as the last person to present. I got through my presentation with no idea how it went, because I was distracted and shaken by nearly missing it altogether. After the session, I then uploaded my slide deck and ran as fast as I could in the direction of coffee.

Following the event, I received constructive feedback from my colleagues and continued with my networking. Later that afternoon, I logged in to my email and saw a message that I had received on a social media site from an intern at SlideShare, informing me that they would review and consider my slides. I received the following message from SlideShare the next day: "Your Slide is trending in your area."

SlideShare featured my slides on the main page of their website. For a better perspective on what that means, consider these SlideShare user statistics:

- » SlideShare has 70 million users.
- » SlideShare averages 400,000 new slides per month (or 100,000 per week).
- » As of December 2013, SlideShare was averaging 189 million page views per month.

In other words, I hit the SlideShare jackpot. The intern made my wish come true. When I returned to Los Angeles after the conference, I received another jackpot email. A well-known publication had written about the conference and listed the most popular slides from the event. They described my deck as "wildly popular," with the most downloaded slides from the conference.

From then on, I was asked to speak everywhere. I now average about seventy-five invitations to speak per year, and I speak at twenty to twenty-five conferences and events annually. In three years, I have spoken at more than seventy conferences all over the world. That SlideShare presentation drew a lot of attention, contributing greatly to my overnight success as a speaker.

The following year, I spoke at the same conference that had launched my speaking career. Again I was nervous, imagining that my success was only due to convincing someone to feature me. But I hadn't actually convinced them; I had just asked them to consider me.

As I entered the conference hall, I was stopped by a woman who said something that instantly calmed my nerves and affirmed my legitimacy. "I was here last year and saw your presentation about Pinterest, and it changed my life," she said. "I never thought of marketing that way before, and you explained it so clearly." I was speechless with happiness.

I had not played by the same set of rules as many others, but taking that extra step to ensure that the content I created would be seen had made all the difference. Ultimately, SlideShare featured my slides because they found them useful—the same reason that people downloaded them.

The point of this story is not about overcoming self-doubt but about getting your work out there in front of other people. Many of us avoid putting our work in front of mass audiences, believing that "the work will show for itself." This approach no longer works. We can't assume that our work is so good that it will stand out in the crowd and be discovered by people who may not understand what we do.

Flash forward one year later, when I received an email from a literary agency in New York. I took a call with the agent that day, having no idea what to expect. I thought she may have wanted help with marketing clients or herself, and I was prepared to answer her questions.

But instead, she asked if I had ever considered writing a book. She said that she had found me on SlideShare, where she noticed that my slides had a lot of views. She could see that my audience was very interested in my unique approach to digital marketing. With the kind of reach I had on SlideShare, she thought that publishers would love to work with me. And that was the beginning of how I came to this line in my book and how you came to be reading it.

THE INVERSE APPROACH TO PERSONAL BRANDING

To think of personal branding and self-promotion from an inverse perspective means to think of things out of order, in a different direction, against the grain.

If we want to get noticed on social media, many of us post a lot of stuff about ourselves: pictures, videos, comments, blogs, and so on. These are all useful after someone has taken notice of us—but what about before?

To understand the importance of the inverse approach to personal branding, work-life, and self-promotion, we first need to see the problem with the common approach. Following is a list of common statements I hear whenever I talk with people about expanding their brand, followed by its inverse.

Assumption: If you work hard, people will notice you.

Inverse: You aren't working hard enough if no one notices you.

Assumption: If you ask questions, people will think you are stupid.

Inverse: You are stupid if you don't ask questions.

Assumption: If you want someone to notice you, you have to spend time where they are.

Inverse: If you want someone to notice you, spend time where they want to be.

Assumption: When you are given an award, the company giving you the award will promote it.

Inverse: People are often given awards in the hope that they will promote the award and the company that gave it to them.

Assumption: You should create and share content that people care about.

Inverse: You should ask people what they care about and use their responses to create content that they will share.

Assumption: If I write my opinion in an article and it turns out to be wrong, everyone will think I'm stupid.

Inverse: If people think your opinion is wrong, they are mistaken; an opinion is an opinion, not a fact.

Think about something negative you are telling yourself every day that is bringing you down and then think of its inverse. If your assumption sounds even worse this way, then you may need to adjust your way of thinking. You have to start asking yourself the hard questions so that you can approach your self-promotion in an inverse way.

REVERSE STALKING: DO YOU SEE ME NOW?

If you want people to see what you have done and all of your wonderful successes, you have to tell them. If you don't want to, there are other ways. Companies can boost their marketing efforts and company culture by applying some (but not all) of these tactics.

First, if you are on LinkedIn, did you know that you can easily and quickly download your contacts into a beautiful Excel spreadsheet? Here's how to do this:

1. Log in to LinkedIn.

2. Click the Network icon at the top of your LinkedIn home page.

3.   Click Your Connections on the left rail.

4.   Click "Manage synced and imported contacts" near the top right of the page.

5.   Under Advanced Actions on the right rail, click Export Contacts. You may be prompted to sign in to your account.

6.   Click Request Archive.

7.   You will receive an email at the Primary Email address listed in your account, including a link where you can download your list of connections.

Your contacts will appear in a tidy file, which you can then organize by job title, company, name, location, or connections. (The steps for how to download your contacts can be found verbatim on the LinkedIn Help page.)

ONE MORE HACK

Read the blog, updated terms of service, and help pages of social media sites for accurate, relevant information about them, and think about how you can use what you know in an inverse way. You can find a digital list of the most relevant social media information pages for each site at: cynthialive.com/platform.

Never send a mass email to this list of contacts. They did not subscribe to your email list, so be considerate. Actually, it is more about conversion rates than about internet etiquette. What are conversion rates? Conversion rates happen on the internet and on social media when the action you want to be performed by another person is performed. If you want to create conversions, you need to have great content that can capture the interest and direct the intent of the person you distribute that content to. No one wants your spam, and it is not the best use of this list.

What you can do with these email addresses is technically not allowed on most social media sites, but remember, in a three-way relationship we need to consider how everyone will benefit. The social media platforms want to make money, you want to build a brand, and the contact doesn't want to be spammed. There is a solution, but, yes, technically it breaks the rules.

OUT OF SIGHT, OUT OF MIND

The importance of your contacts is not to see whom you know but to assess who knows you. It makes a huge difference to connect with people when you know who they are, and in return they have a clear idea of who you are, what you do, and what you need or want.

Have you ever had one of those moments when you ask a small group of people if they know a type of service person or company; for example, "Does anyone know a good house cleaner in West Los Angeles?" Immediately you get several responses, usually followed with, "They are amazing," or "I have used them for years." These referrals are top of the mind. These are the people who represent a specific thing, message, or movement.

When I started my career in social media, I had a difficult time getting people in the company to listen to me. I would sit in meetings with engineers, executives, and others, and I would constantly be overlooked. I knew there was a chance that the company could go out of business, and that I wanted to take on side projects (and start my own agency one day). But how would I ever manage to project my agency brand, build trust, and gain clients if I couldn't even get my coworkers to listen to what I had to say?

Some of the people I worked with couldn't even remember my name, so they often called me "the social media girl." Every time they had a question about social media, they'd say, "Where is the social media girl?" I knew I had to do something to make myself more visible than just as the young woman who might be an intern.

I decided that I would embrace being the social media girl. That way I could first test my theories at the office, and when I opened my own agency, I would have a working template.

I started by going online and buying the largest pair of fake glasses I could find, from a company I had never heard of. (I never needed glasses in my life, but I had always wanted to wear them.) I had noticed the recent trend of oversized glasses among hipster men in East Los Angeles. I had always felt slightly intimidated by their confidence—especially in their ability to do whatever it was they did. If this could work for them, I thought, maybe it could work for me.

I bought the big glasses, a pair of loafers, and some button-down shirts that I buttoned all the way up. I was the social media girl, and this was my new look. When I went to work, my new communication strategy was to lead with facts, appear disinterested, and always overdeliver. I would focus positive attention on employees and stare blankly at my bosses. This was my way of trying to get the ear of the executives. My rationale was that it was the exact opposite of what I was currently doing, and what I was currently doing wasn't working.

People who hear this story ask whether I felt as if I was not myself by doing this. For one thing, I was never really myself as an entry-level employee: I was just playing the part. Do you know how many times I wanted to tell off someone in a meeting, or walk out? But instead, I would nod in agreement or have a carefully worded discussion in front of everyone. Although that is not who I am, everyone was okay with that being the "real" me. Another thing is that my clothes and my fake glasses were a choice. They were not me deciding to be someone I am not; they were me deciding to change my work appearance. I had never wanted to wear slacks, pencil skirts, and button-ups. I had just returned from traveling the world, and the office vibe was not my thing. Back then, I didn't even want to wear shoes. But I had to do it and abide by a certain dress code.

I find it amusing that if a person wears clothes that are outside of their norm in order to achieve a goal, they may be perceived as a fake. But if a person wears clothes or a uniform they would not normally wear because an employer wants them to, they are perceived as doing their job. Ultimately, with my choice of how to change my communication style, I was moving closer to the person and interaction style that felt right to me. So I didn't feel like a fake or a fraud; I felt strategic.

I went to work the first day with my new look and my giant glasses on. I sat in the usual weekly meetings, and no one said anything about the glasses or commented on my look. Instead, I was invited to help videotape a live-streamed event with the technical crew. I had worked for this company off and on for more than two years, and no one had ever asked me to help with events before (the fun part of the job). Now I had people sending me messages on Google Talk (this was before Slack). I was put in charge of a new game that was released. I began helping with content for the front page of the website. (The company was a live-streaming social network with about nine million registered users.) I became the cool kid—one of the people others listened to and asked questions of. The less I said or acted as if I cared, the more confident I appeared, and the more I was able to participate.

The company closed about four months after my transformation into the social media girl. At that point, I had started to build out social media profiles. I took a selfie with my phone to use as a headshot, and I created a blog. By the time the company went under, I had already taken on side work and launched a brand called The Social Media Girl.

The Social Media Girl.
#TheSMGirl

I wanted to look as much like a cartoon character as possible, so that people would see the message, the goal, and the brand before they saw another twentysomething intern type. At this point I was nearly twenty-six, and I needed to make real money.

When we got the news that it was over, I was laid off along with about forty other people. It was terrible. Some of them had worked at the company since the beginning, had families, and genuinely loved what they had created. We were all given two-weeks severance pay because we were a social media content company, and we had to help the users gather their content before we closed. If we stayed the two weeks, we could come by to pick up our severance checks and shake hands with the former CEO. Until that handshake, he had never uttered a word to me, even though my cubicle was directly in front of his office.

I worked at my next job, a company called RankLab, for almost six months before anyone asked me if my glasses were real or not. Back then we were just five people sitting around a conference table, so we all had a good laugh.

The point of the story is that you have to shift your own mindset before you can shift someone else's. If that means dressing in fake glasses for a few months to avoid looking like everyone else, why not? If this were a play and you were cast as an executive, you would be expected to dress the part. In fact, if you know anyone who has become an executive, watch and see if they start to shift the way they dress to look the part.

Appearing as a social media girl, calling myself the social media girl, and posting online about social media positioned me to attract anyone looking for social media anything. I was the all-encompassing social media resource. I ended up getting written about in social media publications, appearing in many searches, and being offered a lot of jobs. I was top of mind.

When I wanted to shift my personal brand from social media girl to digital marketing strategist, I needed a growth strategy. As cool as social media was, I was doing more, and I wanted more. I decided that I was going to try a new look. I ditched the glasses, cut my bangs, and let my natural hair color come in. I was already doing work outside of social media, but I needed to find a way to shift my online presence. Everyone still knew me as the social media girl at work. I was ready to stop taking calls on that topic, because I wanted to become top of mind for digital marketing strategy.

I had a friend take a picture of me looking busy, I updated my profile bios and images to say digital marketing, and I shifted my brand all at once. I didn't want it to be a slight change, so I didn't change anything until everything was ready to change. I changed the topics I wrote about from social media to business and marketing. Whenever I released a new article or was interviewed about marketing or business, I would take that LinkedIn mailing list (that we downloaded earlier) along with all my other emails and upload them as a custom audience on Facebook. I spent next to nothing to make sure that everyone who knew me saw me talking about business and marketing.

What happens when you use content about you—strategic content focused on what you want to do and your brand message—that is not produced by you? People start taking you and your efforts more seriously. I would take this content, even a blog article or podcast interview, and use the advertising tools that Facebook gave me, along with the emails that LinkedIn gave me, to add my new content to the news feed of the people I knew. Since then, other social media advertising platforms, such as LinkedIn, Google (including YouTube and Gmail), Twitter, and Instagram, have opened up to allow the use of emails to target audiences.

The way it works is that you need an email list of about one thousand people who have email accounts registered with the social media site. Then you upload your email list and create an ad. The more targeted your ad, the less expensive it will be to run. This is one way to follow people all over the web. We live in our own worlds, and when we see someone with a blog on LinkedIn, an article on Facebook, and a video on YouTube, we assume that we are seeing them everywhere, simply because we failed to note the first or second time we saw them. Eventually we conclude that this person must be doing something right in his or her area of expertise because they are getting so much attention. Instead of realizing that the content is probably circulating among a small group of people who live in a big world, we assume we are seeing what most people are seeing. This pushes the person we see everywhere to top of mind.

This strategy for following people all over the web with your content can be very useful. For example, employers can write stories about their employees and then run ads to their target audiences with this content. It is an easy and inexpensive way to stay top of mind with people and help create opportunity that comes to you instead of your having to constantly chase it.

HOW IMPORTANT IS IT TO BE TOP OF MIND?

How important is it to be top of mind when you are seeking a job, running a company, or building a brand? It turns out that it might well be the most important thing of all. In a March 2017 article in *Fast Company*, Robert Coombs wrote about building a bot to apply to thousands of jobs at once, and the insights he gained by doing so.[20] Robert Coombs was a director at a national nonprofit organization. He loved his team but had started to notice that they no longer needed his direction as much as they once did. He wasn't in a hurry to get a job because he loved where he worked, but he thought maybe it was time to start looking around for one.

He started by applying manually (and slowly) to a few job openings at major tech companies such as Slack, Facebook, and Google. He soon realized that not only was he up against people in the tech space, so his résumé probably wouldn't jump to the top of the pile, but also that robots were reading his résumé first (and robots read every word).

There is a tool called applicant tracking systems (ATS) that automatically filters out job applicants and candidates based on keywords, skills, former employers, years of experience, and the schools they attended. When he realized that he was working with robots, Robert decided to build his own robot to help level the playing field. It was a genius move.

His article explains how he created the bot. First, you should know that Robert is not an engineer: his experience in technology included playing around and learning to automate a few processes, such as social media, data processing, and web content. According to Robert, he cobbled together a Rube Goldberg–ian contraption of crawlers, spreadsheets, and scripts to automate his job-application process and modestly referred to it as his robot. He used his tools and spreadsheets to create a robot that aggregated hiring managers' contact information and then submitted customized emails with his résumé and a personalized cover letter. "Soon, I was imagining myself telling the story of how I'd turned my job search into a super-precise job firehose," he wrote.

From there, he tracked the number of times his cover letter, résumé, and LinkedIn profile were viewed. He tracked all of the email responses that he received from the companies he applied to. In the first round, Robert applied to 1,300 jobs in about a half hour, all located in the Midwest. Considering that he lived in New York, he knew that wasn't going to work. So he went back to the drawing board and found a sweet spot for his automated application process. For him and his robot, the magic formula ultimately culled 538 jobs in his area over a period of three months.

The results that Robert found were astonishing. He was using A/B testing (to compare two versions of a web page) in his automated emails and cover letters. In one test, he even admitted that his cover letter was written by a robot. His robot was built to optimize, change, and learn so that the next cover letter and email would perform better. It turned out that it doesn't matter. Not only are people not reading your cover letters; neither are the robots.

Robert's article clearly indicated that he was upset—as many people who are looking for jobs should be. Robert was targeting companies that were more likely to use robots to read his résumé. He wanted to find a way to get through their algorithm; however, the keywords that robots targeted were the only thing that really mattered. They were looking for proof that he had worked at a tech company before, and if they didn't find it, he had little chance of manipulating the system.

Let's look at other factors that may have made this an impossible task for Robert. In 2014, Meta Brown and Giorgio Topa from the Federal Reserve Bank of New York, and Elizabeth Setren from the Massachusetts Institute of Technology wrote a research paper, titled "Do Informal Referrals Lead to Better Matches? Evidence from a Firm's Employee Referral System."[21] Their study found that in the United States, 30 to 50 percent of hires come from referrals. Applicants who have been referred are more than four times as likely to be hired over non-referred applicants. According to another study cited in Robert's article, referrals fill 85 percent of all critical job openings in the United States. This means that only 15 percent of the critical jobs are left for people who apply without a referral.

Robert's article also considers whether people who fill out LinkedIn applications actually get jobs. One person he asked was Amy Segelin, president of Chaloner, an executive communications recruiting firm. She told him, "Out-of-the-box hires rarely happen through LinkedIn applications. They happen when someone influential meets a really interesting person and says, 'Let's create a position for you.'"

In a podcast for NPR's *All Things Considered*, the host interviewed Matt Youngquist, president of Career Horizons. "At least 70 percent, if not 80 percent, of jobs are not published," said Youngquist. "And yet most people—they are spending 70 or 80 percent of their time surfing the net versus getting out there, talking to employers, taking some chances [and] realizing that the vast majority of hiring is friends and acquaintances hiring other trusted friends and acquaintances." This means that online job applicants are seeing only the 20 to 30 percent of jobs that are advertised, and they have to fight to find the small percentage of jobs that are filled by people who are not referred.

In this podcast, NPR also interviewed Ashley Stirrup, vice president of product marketing at Taleo. Stirrup said that larger, more known companies average six times as many applicants per year as there are employees in the company. If you do the math, you'll realize that competition is steep, opportunities are few, and being top of mind matters far more than most people realize.

The question we should all be asking is not, "How do you stand out in a job application process?" Rather, it's "How do you stand out to hiring managers and their networks before you even apply?"

So now that you know jobs aren't being posted and referrals are everything, you have to change your strategy. How do you get chosen for a particular position? How do you end up being the employee who gets the job, the speaker who lands the keynote, or the agency that wins the big account?

According to both *Adweek* and a 2015 Jobvite study about the Social Recruiting Survey, 92 percent of recruiters use social media to find high-quality candidates.[22] How could that be, when we know that so many jobs come through referrals? The keywords here are "uses social media to *find* high-quality candidates"—not to help *them* find jobs. Social media websites are not being used nearly as much to cast a wide net and catch new employees by advertising jobs; they are being used to find the employee who appears right for the job. These are people who have jobs already, and other companies are coming in to try to scoop them up.

Why would we need to use job advertisements if we can find our ideal person, offer them more money than they're making, and call it a day? The fact is that we do not, and no one does. Robert's study was an interesting one, but I think he was looking at it backward. Instead of using a bot to identify and change keywords in online job applications or profile pages to try to get past the robots, he should have been keyword optimizing his LinkedIn profile (using words that recruiters are looking for when searching for ideal candidates) and connecting with the friends of recruiters, or people at the companies he was most interested in. Even from a purely psychological standpoint, you never want to be the one asking for something. You always want to position yourself to be the one who is asked.

Instead of reaching out to the hiring manager, reach out to an employee at the company, ask for a call, and then ask for a referral. It is more effective and easier than ever to find and contact an employee at a company. The *Adweek* article states that "employee referrals are also important to the recruiting process, with 78 percent of recruiters finding their best candidates that way."

Staying top of mind, even if it requires you to game the advertising arms of social media companies, is absolutely okay and even necessary. Spend a little more time in groups, write a couple of blogs on your LinkedIn page, and connect with people. Your brand, when it comes to getting more work and recognition, is 30 to 50 percent dependent on your network, how they perceive you, and what they know about you.

11 YOU CAN NEVER BE A PROPHET IN YOUR OWN LAND

If you think that standing up for what you believe in and thinking out loud can have harmful effects on your income, your career, and your life, then you are not thinking for yourself. You are thinking about how other people will perceive your thoughts. You don't have to be outrageous; you don't have to be combative; you just have to be focused and fearless.

Someone out there in the world already hates you. You may or may not know each other, but they hate you because of your sex, race, nationality, lack of money, possession of money, because of how you voted, because you didn't vote, and so on. Is that terrible? Yes, of course. Does it change your day-to-day life? No, because you probably don't know who they are, or you just flat out avoid them. People hate us for things that are beyond our control. We cannot avoid being hated or prevent bias toward us, but we can avoid being affected by it. We can move past it and do our own thing. Bias is everywhere—even in ourselves—whether or not we are aware of it or acknowledge it.

What do we really have to worry about by being too authentic? People care about how you make them feel and how you might benefit them, far more than they care about what you do. That is not selfishness; it is a human trait. How many times have you been tagged in a group photo online, and when you got the image, the first person you looked at in the photo wasn't yourself? Probably rarely or never, like most of us. We worry so much about what other people think of us without stopping to consider that they're usually thinking about themselves.

BREAK THROUGH THE BOUNDARIES OF FAMILIARITY

As you grow your brand, you will start to feel resistance from people you know and love. It is not that they don't want you to succeed; it is that they don't want the relationship to change. People dislike change in general, and as you become more recognizable and more of a thought-leader, the people closest to you may fear your development. However, this might only last for a short time before everyone accepts the change.

The people closest to you are too familiar with you to really understand or know how to support you as you grow. This can be stifling to your growth. If you try to see yourself as the people around you do, you won't know if or when you are capable of something greater. This can be true in a family environment, work environment, relationship, or even a friendship. When you pursue goals beyond what you have historically done, the people closest to you may not see the opportunities or your abilities as clearly as an outsider would. We are all more attractive to people outside of our immediate circle. This is based on the law of familiarity: the longer you are around something, the more you take it for granted.

Having worked with executives and leaders from around the world, I have noticed a few significant differences in perspectives on personal branding:

» People who are coming from long-term business partnerships or who work within organizations tend to shy away from the idea of personal branding; they share success with their peers and are overly humble and modest about their achievements.

» People who are out of their geographical elements tend to thrive in personal branding; they're open to change, they're not limited by their immediate networks, and they don't face as much discouraging feedback from people they know.

» People who have been in long-term careers tend to undervalue their abilities and avoid attention.

RESISTANCE FROM PEOPLE WHO DON'T LOVE YOU

You will be sure to find people who dislike you everywhere you go. As you build your brand and start using your voice more, you will find more people who think they dislike you. Instead of retreating or downplaying your success, you will have to push through the feeling of wanting to succeed in front of your haters. You will have to ignore them or learn to kill them with kindness.

When people say and do negative things to others, I have found that it is usually because of a negative or insecure feeling they have about themselves. But sometimes people just don't agree with you, and that is okay; they don't have to. As my grandmother often says, "I may disagree with what you say, but I will defend 'til death your right to say it."

If you spend too much time defending yourself from people who disagree with you, then you will lose valuable time needed to achieve your goals. I always like to squash these situations by responding,

"I'm sorry you feel that way. I hope you have a nice day." Or I respond by acknowledging something positive about them from their bio. People can't stay mad at a stranger who compliments them—at least not for long.

DON'T THINK YOU CAN HANDLE THE PRESSURE OF YOUR HATERS?

I get it. Some people are scared and nervous at the prospect of going against the grain, exposing themselves and their ideas to the world, and risking what could happen if they fail. Anyone who has seen the "Mean Tweets" segment on *Jimmy Kimmel Live!* can understand how it might be difficult for people to build a brand and promote themselves. It can open you up to negative feedback and discrimination.

Though I have received only a small amount of negative commentary and email, it has happened. Once I even had a troll email my job because I had written a story about a D-list celebrity who was trolled online. The trolls turned into crazies, who emailed my employer saying that they had hired a "gadget girl" and suggesting that I should be fired. I wasn't fired, but I was not allowed to walk to my car alone after work.

NEXT TIME YOU THINK THE CARDS ARE STACKED AGAINST YOU, THINK OF SARAH BREEDLOVE

Sarah Breedlove is considered the first female self-made millionaire. At the time of her death, she was worth $600,000, which would be about $8 million today. Sarah Breedlove was not an ordinary entrepreneur or millionaire by male or female standards. If you have heard of her, you probably know her as Madame C.J. Walker.

She was an American entrepreneur and philanthropist, as well as a political and social activist. She is considered the world's most successful female entrepreneur of her time and one of the most successful African American business owners of all time.

Sarah was born into a family near Delta, Louisiana, on December 23, 1867, the youngest of six children. She was the first person in her family to be born into freedom after the Emancipation Proclamation was issued by President Abraham Lincoln in 1863.

Her mother died when Sarah was only five, and her father passed away two years later. She was an orphan at the age of seven. At age ten and with no formal education, she moved in with her sister and got a job as a housekeeper. At age fourteen, she married a man named Moses McWilliams, presumably to escape her abusive brother-in-law. Imagine that you have no education, both of your parents are dead, you work as a maid, you are a black woman living in the South in the years after the Emancipation Proclamation, your sister's husband abuses you, and to escape the abuse you end up married at age fourteen.

In 1885, when Sarah was eighteen, she gave birth to a daughter, Lelia McWilliams. Two years later, her husband, Moses, passed away. Now she was a single mother, who needed to quickly figure out what to do in order to take care of her daughter. So Sarah and Lelia moved to St. Louis, Missouri, to be near Sarah's three older brothers. There she took a job as a laundress, earning less than a dollar a day.

Sarah's goals were clear and simple: to make enough money for her daughter to go to school and get a formal education. For fun, Sarah would sing in the church choir and visit her brothers at the barbershop where they worked.

As she aged, Sarah began to experience the hair loss and dandruff common for African American women at that time. This was in part caused by the harsh hair-care products they used, many of which included ingredients such as lye that were found in soaps for washing clothes. Other factors that caused scalp issues and hair loss were a lack of indoor plumbing, infrequent showering, and poor diet. Whatever the reasons, Sarah was experiencing this problem, and she wasn't happy about it.

She decided to take a job as a commission agent for Annie Turnbo Malone, the owner of an African American hair-care company. Since Sarah had hair and scalp problems of her own, she was very interested in these products. She began to learn about them and then to alter them. Eventually she realized that she had a better formula, and she started to develop her own product line. During this time, Sarah also married and divorced her second husband, John Davis. Sarah knew how to think for herself, both professionally and personally.

In 1905, while still working for Malone, Sarah moved with her daughter to Colorado, where she met Charles Joseph Walker, the man who would become her third husband. After they married in 1906, Sarah took her husband's last name and started her own company with him. She changed her name to Madam C. J. Walker, to match the goal of the business. The title "Madam" was inspired by successful entrepreneurs and pioneers in the French beauty industry. Madam C. J. Walker began selling her products door-to-door, teaching other black women how to care for the style and health of their hair.

Later that year, Sarah put her daughter in charge of shipping products for the orders that she and her husband took as they traveled through the United States, selling their products door-to-door. The following year, they opened a beauty salon and school in Pittsburgh, Pennsylvania, called Lelia College of Beauty Culture, to train future "beauty culturists." The couple would eventually open another salon and school in Harlem, New York.

Just four years after launching her door-to-door business, Sarah opened her own manufacturing company in Indianapolis. Between 1911 and 1919, Madam C. J. Walker's company employed thousands of women to sell her products. The women wore white or black skirts and carried black bags. They went door-to-door to sell not only the product but also the brand message.

All of the women Madam C. J. Walker employed as beauty culturists were taught "the Walker Method," including how to budget and open their own businesses. In 1917, she created state and local clubs for her sales agents to participate in. She named her association the National Beauty Culturists and Benevolent Association of Madam C. J. Walker Agents (predecessor to the Madam C. J. Walker Beauty Culturists Union of America). The association held events and national gatherings, and gave awards to the saleswomen who sold the most, brought in the most new sales agents, and made the largest donations to their local charities.

Sarah Walker was also a philanthropist and visionary. In 1912, she spoke to the annual gathering of the National Negro Business League (NNBL) from the convention floor: "I am a woman who came from the cotton fields of the South. From there, I was promoted to the washtub. From there, I was promoted to the cook kitchen. And from there, I promoted myself into the business of manufacturing hair goods and preparations. I have built my own factory on my own ground."

At the same conference the following year, Madam C. J. Walker was the keynote speaker. Her philanthropic work was extensive and effective. She donated to the building fund for the Indianapolis Young Men's Christian Association (YMCA). She also provided scholarship funds to the Tuskegee Institute, Indianapolis House, and the Bethel African Methodist Episcopal Church, among other organizations.

Sarah Breedlove not only worked *for* the black community, she also worked to create an acceptance of it. She moved to New York City in 1918, where she became the assistant secretary for Negro affairs of the United States Department of War. She went on to become more and more political, giving speeches on political, social, and economic issues at conventions and events sponsored by black institutions.

Sarah Breedlove built an empire, empowered a community, brought positive change, and developed an incredible personal brand in a time when women had few rights and black women had even fewer. To give you an idea of the kind of world she was up against, she never had the right to vote in America despite her influence. Sarah passed away in May 1919, and women were granted the right to vote in June 1919 (ratified August 1920).

So the next time you start to tell yourself that you have it rough or that something is impossible, think of Sarah "Madam C.J. Walker" Breedlove. She stood behind her beliefs, her drive, and her love for community to build something out of nothing. She is a true role model for success and perseverance. She is the kind of person we should honor, and everyone should know her name.

YOUR PERSONAL BRAND NEEDS A GROWTH STRATEGY

Let's say you have already reached the place where you have a brand message, a website, media, your own byline; you are speaking at events, and your social media is on its way. You are the top person to call when someone needs a wealth manager, a real-estate agent, a doctor, a life coach, a commercial actor, or whatever you are. Congratulations!—but now what? That's right: what's next? You can't keep doing the same thing over and over. You will get bored, the world will change, and so will your audience.

Think about what happens when child actors grow up, and their audiences grow up, too. When I was young, I was obsessed with Lance Bass from NSYNC. I watched all of the band's videos and bought all of their CDs (yes, CDs). Now that I've grown up, the only NSYNC member who has remained relevant is Justin Timberlake. He got into tech investing with Myspace, he started acting and producing, he had a solo music career, and he kept on changing. He changed his appearance, his message, and the way he delivered his message. Miley Cyrus is another great example: she went from country to outrageous overnight. That was the right next move for her personal brand to make. Were people concerned? Yes. Were they upset? Yes. Did they get over it? Of course they did.

When you are ready to grow your brand, evolve, and move on to the next thing, it is crucial that you do it all at once. If you try to gradually implement change for your brand, you will create confusion and inconsistency. You have to plan the change and then make it happen quickly. Go back to the drawing board, and think about where you are now and where you want to go. Create a new brand statement, a new look for your website, and updated bios that emphasize the new you. When you are all prepared . . . boom! You change everything in a day. Just like that, you flip a switch. People will definitely notice—they always do—and they will have opinions about your new image. But you have to trust your gut and remember that you are not living for anyone else's amusement. The reason you need to make such a fast transition is to avoid confusion.

Get out of your safety bubble. There are people who have no idea who you are. The longer you sit in the small world of influence you have created around yourself, the more out of touch you will become. Don't hang on to that job you quit four years ago. Don't speak at the same conferences every year on the same topics. Change it up. Every industry changes, even yours. If you keep speaking as a topic expert about something that you and your industry have outgrown, you are no better than the political pundits who have no real experience in politics.

Don't sit back and watch less-experienced people take your seat at the table. If you are more experienced, more knowledgeable, and more qualified, then you won't have to compete for a seat at the table. But you will have to ask for one. Don't practice humility so much that you become prideful in your humility. The world needs more real experts to be heard so that fewer fake experts can be heard.

When you settle into that new area of expertise, it will be a shock to your system, because you will realize that not everyone knows who you are. Some of the people are new, the conversation has shifted, and you find yourself feeling as if you are starting over. You will want to run back to that safe place, but don't do it. If you have a pre-existing brand, pivoting to grow your brand and your reach is not starting over: it is expanding your network. Before you know it, the question you will hear most often is, "What do you do now?" People will always ask that question whenever they see someone who has multiple exemplary career paths.

NOTES

Chapter One

1. Joris Lammers, Janka I. Stoker, Floor Rink, and Adam D. Galinsky, "To Have Control Over or to Be free From Others? The Desire for Power Reflects a Need for Autonomy," *Personality and Social Psychology Bulletin,* 42, no. 4 (March 16, 2016): 498–512, https://doi.org/10.1177/0146167216634064.

2. United States Mint, *2014 Annual Report*, 2014, https://www .usmint.gov/wordpress/wp-content/uploads/2016/06/2014Annua lReport.pdf.

3. Margalit Fox, "Gary Dahl, Inventor of the Pet Rock, Dies at 78," *New York Times*, March 31, 2015, https://www.nytimes.com/ 2015/04/01/us/gary-dahl-inventor-of-the-pet-rock-dies-at-78. html.

4. Shannon Gupta, "Nordstrom's Leather-Wrapped Rock Sold Out Online," *CNN Money*, December 8, 2016, http://money.cnn .com/2016/12/07/news/companies/nordstrom-rock-sold-out/ index.html.

5. Alice Dubin and Chris Serico, "That Apple You Just Bought Might Be a Year Old—But Does It Matter?" *Today*, October 13, 2014, https://www.today.com/food/apple-you-just-bought-might-be-year-old-does-it-2D80207170.

Chapter Two

6. Destin Sandlin, "This Experiment Shows Why You Should Put YOUR Oxygen Mask on First," *ScienceAlert*, August 5, 2016, https://www.sciencealert.com/this-crazy-experiment-shows-why-you-should-put-your-oxygen-mask-on-first.

Chapter Three

7.   Eric Schmidt, Jonathan Rosenberg, and Alan Eagle, "How Google Attracts the World's Best Talent," *Fortune*, September 4, 2014, http://fortune.com/2014/09/04/how-google-attracts-the-worlds-best-talent.

Chapter Six

8.   New England Historical Society, The *Boston Herald* Rumor Clinic of World War II, http://www.newenglandhistoricalsociety.com/the-boston-herald-rumor-clinic-of-world-war-ii.

9.   Gordon W. Allport and Leo Postman. *The Psychology of Rumor*, Henry Holt and Company (New York, NY: 1947).

10.   Nicholas DiFonzo and Duncan Watts, "How Do Rumors Get Started?" interview by Joe Palca, *Science*, NPR, November 3, 2006, audio and transcript, https://www.npr.org/templates/transcript/transcript.php?storyId=6429833.

11.   Christopher Paul and Miriam Matthews, "The Russian 'Firehose of Falsehood' Propaganda Model: Why It Might Work and Options to Counter It," RAND Corporation, 2016, https://www.rand.org/pubs/perspectives/PE198.html.

12.   Eric Anderson, Erika H. Siegel, Eliza Bliss-Moreau, and Lisa Feldman Barrett, "The Visual Impact of Gossip," *Science*, 332, no. 6036 (June 17, 2011): 1446–48, https://doi.org/10.1126/science.1201574.

13.   Kevin Koo, Zita Ficko, and E. Ann Gormley, "Unprofessional Content on Facebook Accounts of US Urology Residency Graduates," *BJU International*, April 9, 2017, https://doi.org/10.1111/bju.13846.

14.   Maksym Gabielkov, Arthi Ramachandran, Augustin Chaintreau, and Arnaud Legout, "Social Clicks: What and Who Gets Read on Twitter?" *Inventeurs du Monde Numérique*, June 2016, https://hal.inria.fr/hal-01281190.

Chapter Seven

15. Wu Youyou, Michal Kosinski, and David Stillwell, "Computer-Based Personality Judgments Are More Accurate Than Those Made by Humans," *Proceedings of the National Academy of Sciences of the United States of America*, January 12, 2015, https://doi.org/10.1073/pnas.1418680112.

16. Andrew S. Rosen, "Correlations, Trends and Potential Biases among Publicly Accessible Web-Based Student Evaluations of Teaching: A Large-Scale Study of RateMyProfessors.com Data," *Assessment & Evaluation in Higher Education*, 43, no. 1 (January 8, 2017): 31–44, https://doi.org/10.1080/02602938.2016.1276155.

17. Jordan Golson, "Tesla Is the Most Valuable US Carmaker Because of Hope, Not Results," *The Verge*, April 10, 2017, https://www.theverge.com/2017/4/4/15180402/tesla-most-valuable-carmaker-market-capitalization-ford-gm.

18. Johana Bhuiyan, "Uber Admits That It Has Underpaid Tens of Thousands of Drivers in New York Since Late 2014," *Recode*, May 23, 2017, https://www.recode.net/2017/5/23/15681706/uber-travis-kalanick-underpaid-drivers-new-york-city-refund.

19. Evelyn Cheng, "Tesla's First Junk Bond Offering Is a Hit, But Now Elon Musk Must Deliver: 'No More Room for Excuses,'" *CNBC*, August 11, 2017, https://www.cnbc.com/2017/08/11/tesla-debt-offering-raised-to-1-point-8-billion-300-million-more-than-planned-on-high-demand.html.

Chapter Ten

20. Robert Combs, "I Built a Bot to Apply to Thousands of Jobs at Once—Here's What I Learned," *Fast Company*, March 23, 2017, https://www.fastcompany.com/3069166/i-built-a-bot-to-apply-to-thousands-of-jobs-at-once-heres-what-i-learned.

21. Meta Brown, Elizabeth Setren, and Giorgio Topa, "Do Informal Referrals Lead to Better Matches? Evidence from a Firm's Employee Referral System," *Institute for the Study of Labor (IZA)*, May 24, 2014, https://papers.ssrn.com/sol3/papers.cfm?abstract_id=2441471.

22. Matt Singer, "Welcome to the 2015 Recruiter Nation, Formerly Known as the Social Recruiting Survey," Jobvite, September 22, 2015, https://www.jobvite.com/jobvite-news-and-reports/welcome-to-the-2015-recruiter-nation-formerly-known-as-the-social-recruiting-survey.

ACKNOWLEDGMENTS

Building a platform and writing a book require considerable patience, support, and love from the people in your life. I would like to thank all of those who have encouraged me and believed in me: my grandparents (Thomas and Margaret Pacchioli) for being daring; my parents (Margaret and Paul Cadena) for pushing us to be freethinkers; my siblings (Sarah Johnson, Patrick Johnson, Lindsey Johnson, Kayse Cadena, and JP Cadena) for always having my back; my mentors (Abhilash Patel, Mark Goulston, Yael Swerdlow, and Paula Woods) for helping me overcome many hurdles; my best friends (Ashley Legg and Megan McNichol) for always being a phone call away; and my growth-hacking friends (Ben Landis and Aidan Cole) for teaching me their tricks.

I thank my business partner, friend, and bridesman (Zach Binder) for being the best partner anyone could ask for and for always being there to pick up my slack and my head when I need him to, and a special "Thank you" to our team at Bell + Ivy for all their talent, hard work, and continued support, because without them none of this would have been possible.

I thank my fiancé and best friend, Thomas Pancoast, for being my partner in crime, my editor, a great dog-dad to our Poe, and my biggest cheerleader in life.

To the many people who have followed me and listened as my platform was growing: you are the reason all this is possible. Thank you for supporting me.

INDEX

CYNTHIA JOHNSON is the cofounder of the Los Angeles–based branding agency Bell + Ivy and has 1.7 million followers on Twitter (@CynthiaLive). She was named one of the top five personal branding experts in 2017 by *Entrepreneur magazine, Inc.* listed her as one of the 20 digital marketing people to follow, and Mashable named her the third most important marketer to follow on SnapChat (#CyninLA). Johnson sits on the advisory board for The Millennium Alliance, a leading technology, business, and educational advisory firm serving Fortune 1000 C-Level executives. Cynthia is a global keynote speaker and has addressed companies and events such as Alibaba in China, World Government Summit in Dubai, and Global Ventures Summit in Indonesia and Mexico, as well as USC's Marshall School of Business and Stanford's Igniter program. Her work has been featured in *Inc.*, *Forbes*, and *TIME* and she has advised on the social media, branding, and viral campaigns for companies such as Vans, Levi's, and the Susan B. Komen Foundation. Visit cynthialive.com.

All rights reserved. Published in the United States by
Lorena Jones Books, an imprint of the Crown Publishing
Group, a division of Penguin Random House LLC, New York.
www.crownpublishing.com
www.tenspeed.com

Lorena Jones Books and Lorena Jones Books colophon are
trademarks of Penguin Random House, LLC.

Library of Congress Cataloging-in-Publication Data
    Names: Johnson, Cynthia (Marketing consultant), author.
    Title: Platform : the art & science of personal branding /
    Cynthia Johnson.
    Description: First edition. | New York : Lorena Jones Books,
        [2018] | Includes bibliographical references and index.
    Identifiers: LCCN 2018025079
    Subjects: LCSH: Branding (Marketing)
    Classification: LCC HF5415.1255 .J647 2018 | DDC 650.1—dc23
    LC record available at https://lccn.loc.gov/2018025079

Hardcover ISBN: 978-0-399-58137-3

Ebook ISBN: 978-0-399-58139-7

Printed in the United States of America

Design by Annie Marino

Text and illustration on page 95 reprinted with the
permission of Science.

Myers-Briggs Type Indicator® and MBTI® are registered
trademarks of The Myers & Briggs Foundation.

Instant Domain Search® is a registered trademark
of Hartshorne Software, Inc.

10 9 8 7 6 5 4 3 2 1

First Edition